Harumi's Japanese Cooking

Home
The Berkley Publishing Group
Published by the Penguin Group
Penguin Group (USA) Inc.
375 Hudson Street, New York, New York 10014, USA
Penguin Group (Canada), 90 Eglinton Avenue East, Suite 700,
Toronto, Ontario M4P 2Y3, Canada
(a division of Pearson Penguin Canada Inc.)
Penguin Group Ltd., 80 Strand, London WC2R 0RL, England
Penguin Group Ireland, 25 St. Stephen's Green, Dublin 2, Ireland
(a division of Penguin Books Ltd.)
Penguin Group (Australia), 250 Camberwell Road, Camberwell,
Victoria 3124, Australia (a division of Pearson Australia
Group Pty. Ltd.)
Penguin Books India Pvt. Ltd., 11 Community Centre, Panchsheel
Park, New Delhi—110 017, India
Penguin Group (NZ), Cnr. Airborne and Rosedale Roads, Albany,
Auckland 1310, New Zealand
(a division of Pearson New Zealand Ltd.)
Penguin Books (South Africa) (Pty.) Ltd., 24 Sturdee Avenue,
Rosebank, Johannesburg 2196, South Africa

Penguin Books Ltd., Registered Offices: 80 Strand, London
WC2R 0RL, England

Recipe copyright © Harumi Kurihara
Text copyright © Harumi Kurihara and FCI London 2004
Photo copyright © Fuosha Inc.

Designed by Mark Thomson

Editor: Shirley Booth and Akiko Sakaguchi (Japan)
Text: Harumi Kurihara and Sue Hudson
Layout: Annabel Rooker
Project coordination: Sue Hudson and Akiko Sakaguchi
Translation: Tomoko Miyakoda
Photo Research: Hanako Itahashi
Special Thanks: Yutaka Seino and Naomi Ogura

Produced by International Design UK Ltd

All recipes originally published in Fuosha's
Kurihara Harumi's Suteki Recipe in Japan.

PRINTING HISTORY
Original Conran Octopus Limited edition / 2004
Home edition / April 2006

ISBN 1-55788-486-2
Home is a registered trademark of Penguin Group (USA) Inc.

This book has been cataloged with the Library of Congress.

PRINTED IN HONG KONG

10 9 8 7 6 5 4 3

Photo credits:
Norio Ando pp 34, 60, 61, 80, 81, 150, 151
Takeharu Hioki pp 51, 96, 97, 104, 154
Takahiro Imashimizu pp 14, 52, 53, 100, 101
Masao Kudo pp 16, 17, 27, 30, 32, 39, 45, 55, 56, 57, 68, 71–74,
76, 77, 79, 95, 114, 117, 119, 128, 132, 134, 136–138, 158, 159
Miwa Kumon pp 20, 21
Teruaki Nagamine pp 27, 35, 37, 38, 42, 44, 46, 48, 49, 64, 82, 88, 89,
106–109, 115, 139, 144, 152, 153, 155, 157, 158
Hiroyasu Nakano pp 16, 19, 22, 27, 29, 62, 125, 147, 157–159
Kazuaki Nakazato pp 13, 58, 65, 67, 85, 90, 91, 94, 98, 102, 103, 116,
120, 121, 127
Akio Takeuchi pp 5, 41, 86, 92, 110, 113, 122, 127–131, 140–143, 148,
156

Front and back cover: Akio Takeuchi
Back flap:Teruaki Nagamine

Most Home Books are available at special quantity discounts for
bulk purchases for sales promotions, premiums, fund-raising or
educational use. Special books, or book excerpts, can also be
created to fit specific needs.

For details, write: Special Markets, The Berkley Publishing
Group, 375 Hudson Street, New York, New York 10014.

Harumi's Japanese Cooking

Harumi Kurihara

Home

"Take up the challenge and enjoy a meal with all your senses."

Contents

Foreword
Shirley Booth

To understand the cooking of Harumi Kurihara it is necessary to understand the tradition whence it comes – and from which it then, so creatively, departs. Although the underlying principles of Harumi's cooking are rooted in traditional Japanese cuisine, Harumi is a modern Japanese woman. She was born into post-war American-occupied Japan. This was a time of great change, when Japan was being pulled away from its past and its ancient traditions, towards the future – and the west. Food was a very potent symbol of this. After centuries of eating rice and fish the Japanese were now fast being introduced to bread, milk and hamburgers. Nevertheless, the Japanese love and respect for their traditional ways of eating were deep rooted and never went away.

So although Harumi's cooking is not conventional Japanese cuisine in the established sense, its sensibility underlies all she does. It is both her base and her jumping off point.

So what is this tradition? Recognizing and celebrating the changing of the seasons is an important part of Japanese cuisine. We still have a few foods which we associate with the seasons – strawberries, asparagus and pumpkins, perhaps – but in Japan there are countless foods which are specifically meant to stir the senses at a particular time of year: eel in the stifling heat of summer; matsutake mushrooms in autumn;

bamboo shoots in spring. Furthermore, foods are not only eaten in season (frozen food has never been popular in Japan), but the way they are presented imitates the season and thereby celebrates it. For example, in autumn a dish may be garnished with "pine needles," fashioned from deep-fried noodles bound with nori seaweed, or decorated with red maple leaves. In spring, sweet cakes are fashioned into cherry blossom shapes, and dishes are adorned with sprigs of the real thing.

Using only seasonal ingredients naturally means that they will be at their freshest. And the best way to enjoy the freshest foods is to do as little as possible to them. In fact the Japanese have a saying that the best cooking is the least cooking. This is the principle behind eating sashimi, raw fish. With truly fresh fish the Japanese desire to do only one thing with it – eat it – with only a dash of soy sauce and wasabi to tease out its flavor and complement its succulence.

This is the underlying aim of all Japanese cooking techniques – to preserve and enhance the natural flavor of the ingredients. It follows then that the preparation will be simple. And what Harumi has done is to make this preparation even simpler, and to bring it into the twenty-first century. This is the reason for her popularity among millions of modern-day Japanese women. It is also what interests us.

One of the ways that Harumi does this is in her readiness to use off-the-shelf items to make preparation quick and easy. Ready-made sauces, mayonnaise, canned tuna and spicy pastes are all pressed into service.

Another way is Harumi's willingness to harness technology and bend it to her purpose. For her carrot and tuna salad she uses the microwave to cook the carrots because she believes it helps to maintain their crispness better than by boiling them. Harumi believes in encouraging people to cook healthy and delicious food easily and, if using a microwave helps to achieve that, then that's just fine. She is, though, careful to encourage traditional techniques where she feels it makes a significant difference to a dish. She likes to make her basic stock (called dashi) from scratch, using kombu seaweed and dried fish flakes (katsuo bushi).

So, although Harumi's recipes do not entail hours spent working in the kitchen making pine needles from noodles, they encompass the spirit of Japanese cooking. Where she really parts company with the traditional is in the way she enthusiastically embraces new flavors from all over the world. In the past, food in Japan tended to be either washoku – Japanese, or yoshoku – western, and each cuisine was distinct, but Harumi unself-consciously mixes traditional Japanese ingredients with European and Southeast Asian newcomers. Because of the lack of grazing land for cattle in Japan, and because of Buddhist beliefs which forbade the eating of animals, dairy foods have not traditionally been a part of Japanese cuisine. Harumi though is not afraid to add cream to a dish made with miso, and she serves tofu with Gorgonzola and basil. Cream cheese, tomato ketchup – they all have a role in Harumi's kitchen – and all help to make it accessible to those new to Japanese cooking.

Which leaves us with the question of what is Japanese cuisine these days?

Is it the food that's eaten in Japan? When does a food cross over from one national boundary to another? Not many people these days would question the authenticity of tomatoes in Italian and Spanish cuisine; potatoes are synonymous with Northern European cooking; and yet all were once newcomers regarded with suspicion when they were introduced from the new world. In Japan itself beef was similarly abhorred until the middle of the nineteenth century, yet sukiyaki (made with beef) is now one of the most famous Japanese dishes. In a further irony Japanese "curry" came not from India but from England.

What most certainly does mark Harumi's food out as Japanese is the manner of its presentation. Portions are small and served separately on their own plate. Harumi does not insist that you do the same, although she'll encourage you to try, as it is part of the enjoyment of eating.

This then is stylish, unpretentious cooking that's above all eminently doable. It's the type of food that's prepared for Japanese families, parties and restaurants: the everyday food of twenty-first century Japan.

While extolling the virtues of home-cooked food and stylish presentation Harumi's most important message though is to enjoy what you do. Harumi certainly does – being in the kitchen with her is fun. It is this sense of fun and approachability that has made her message one that millions of Japanese women have responded to. She hopes that what she has to offer will now find a willing ear outside of Japan. I'm sure it will.

Introduction
Harumi Kurihara

I was lucky to grow up in a very traditional and beautiful part of Japan, and to have a mother who worked in the home as well as helping with the family business. She looked after my father and us children and she always cooked delicious fresh Japanese food. This family background has always been my inspiration, and it is from my mother that I learned so many important aspects of what to cook and how to eat. My father ran a small printing company, and my mother would cook three times a day. She would get up at five in the morning to ensure that a hot meal was on the table for her family by six. In the evening she cooked a light meal for the employees too. Even though she no longer has to cook for so many, she still gets up early and uses the time while the rice is cooking to prepare the rest of the meal and get ready for the day – this is her personal time. Unlike most Japanese women these days my mother wears a kimono every day, finding it comfortable and easy to wear. I myself have inherited her habit of getting up early and I too relish the peace of early mornings, puttering in my kitchen, creating a harmonious and happy life for my family. In the past, of course, it was quite common for women to spend a lot of time in the kitchen, but these days it's a rarity.

Our home was always full of people; our family, the people working for my father, friends and visitors. My mother would quite often find herself making a meal for around a dozen people, but she always made it look easy and would quietly just get on with it – with each individual dish perfectly prepared.

My mother inspired me to see that although there are many things in life that may seem routine, or even boring, like cooking every day for your family, if you approach it with the right attitude you can achieve great satisfaction. By taking care of detail you can find happiness in small everyday things, which make all the difference to a family who are living in the same house and sharing meals together.

When I look at my mother I feel such tenderness and pride. I am so impressed by her ability to carry on calmly through good times and bad.

Like many Japanese families, we lived by the sea so naturally we ate a lot of fish, but, unusually for those days, we also ate quite a lot of meat. Whatever my mother served was always carefully prepared, using ingredients that we consider important for good health, such as a variety of seaweed, sesame, soy sauce and of course rice. After all, meals cooked for your family aren't simply to fill empty stomachs, but to ensure healthy bodies too.

Now, in my own home I can see the influence of that background; the influence of my parents, and in particular my mother. I too have a home filled with family and visitors. I too rise early to get the house ready for another day , prepare food and cook for my family, to sustain them and to keep them healthy – my main drive comes from cooking for my family and friends.

In the same way I am not interested in decorating my food for the sake of it. Too many cooks these days add gratuitous decoration to their dishes, thinking that it makes the dish look more beautiful, but I don't, and I'm sure this is the reason why my books seem to have had such appeal in Japan.

My recipes and Japanese cuisine

You will find when you come to look at my recipes that I try to make meals from readily available ingredients, the type of things that people already have in their pantry or refrigerator or, indeed, using leftovers. Then I add a twist using some new seasoning, which makes it special. It has simply been the needs of my own family that have driven me to create new and interesting ways to eat familiar food. One of my most popular recipes is my carrot and tuna salad; I created this over twelve years ago and I still receive letters about it. I dressed the salad in a way which just seems to have inspired people. Another example is one of my hamburger recipes – here I added some shavings of burdock (a Japanese root vegetable called gobo) to the meat mixture, giving it a Japanese accent and at the same time adding something healthy.

Of course, the foundation of my cooking is traditional Japanese cuisine, and to learn how to cook Japanese food is to take a voyage to a culture with a different sensibility. The presentation, the variety and the seasonality all mark out Japanese food as a unique cuisine, and, although it looks simple there is complexity in the balance of the seasoning.

Many of my western friends are surprised when they hear of traditional Japanese thinking on variety in eating – we think that you should eat around thirty different types of food a day. That's why one meal contains so many different things. I think if a meal is made up of only a few ingredients it can be very boring – we need to have different flavors and even different textures to create balance and interest. It's worth noting also that this traditional way of eating has been credited with helping the Japanese people stay slim, as well as having many other health benefits.

Rice

The most important ingredient though in nearly every meal is rice. Rice is the center of Japanese culinary life – the most important thing – the main dish.

When you go to buy rice in Japan (or in Asian stores abroad), you'll find a bewildering array of packages and sacks, all seemingly identical but to the connoisseur all subtly different. Japanese rice is short-grained and full of flavor. This type of short-grain rice is easier than the long-grain variety to pick up with chopsticks. I am sure that many Japanese, like myself, could not imagine life without rice.

Tableware and Presentation

Another important thing that you'll notice when looking at a Japanese meal is that it is served on lots of different plates and bowls. Most westerners visiting a Japanese house are astonished by the huge number of dishes crammed into the kitchen cupboards. There are small dishes for soy sauce, long plates for grilled fish, bowls with lids on for miso soup and so on, and, unlike western tableware, the pieces don't have to match.

In addition to ceramics we have glass, lacquer, metal and wooden dishes. In summer we use a lot of glass dishes to provide us with a visual sense of coolness – something you really need in the hot, humid Japanese summers. Lacquer is traditionally used in winter when its soft warmth is so appreciated. Those of you who are familiar with sushi will probably have seen the beautiful wooden plates that are often used to serve it on. Bamboo, which is so prevalent in Japan, is extensively and creatively used. The sheer range of materials reflect the diversity of the cuisine and emphasise the importance of presentation in Japanese meals.

Newcomers to this style of eating are often surprised by the extremely diverse range of dishes used, but I love tableware and one of my greatest pleasures in travelling is scouring antique shops, markets and department stores for unusual ceramics. Some pieces can be made of delicate high-quality bone china or porcelain, while others are made from heavy earthenware, but we relish the contrast created by such a presentation.

In fact, an important part of the cook's job is choosing the best dish for each recipe, as the correct dish will complete the picture of the meal. In common with much of Japanese art, such as sumi-e (the traditional black-and-white brushstroke painting), we believe that simplicity is a key element in beauty. This simplicity also means that each dish holds only a small portion of food so that the dish itself can seen and appreciated. Many of my Japanese friends who travel abroad tell me how shocked they are to see a mountain of food arriving on one plate. They feel overwhelmed by the quantity and see it as almost obscene. No, we prefer to have lots of dishes holding small quantities of each individual recipe.

I divide my own huge collection of dishes into three different groups. There are the dishes that I use every day – easy to use, usually not expensive and easy to replace. Then there are what could be called the "dollhouse" dishes – tiny little plates and bowls which remind me of the small dishes that I would play with as a child. These dishes are typically Japanese and are used for soy sauce, dressings or other condiments. The final group is what I think of as my "reward" dishes. These are plates or bowls that are usually unique and sometimes expensive. I consider that I work hard every day and so occasionally I like to reward myself by indulging my love of beautiful things. Using one of these "reward" dishes makes a meal feel extra special.

I think in the west many people buy themselves one set of matching china and never change it or add to it, despite the inevitable changes in taste and fashion that we experience as an individual and as a society. Over the years my tastes have changed and I enjoy buying new items to use for our meals. At the moment I am using a lot

of oval-shaped dishes as I think they are versatile and attractive for many different types of foods.

In fact, I encourage you to experiment with different shapes – I would become so bored if I could use only round plates. Also experiment with how you use dishes – there is no reason why you shouldn't use them for candles or flowers at a party. Although traditionally we used to say that certain plates must be used for this and another for that I am feeling increasingly liberated from that way of thinking. I think you should use a variety of different tableware at any one time and not be limited too much by the traditional seasonality of tableware. Use your imagination and have fun! I think it is a fantastic way of tapping into your own creativity.

Etiquette
Traditionally in Japan we were encouraged not to talk while eating. Some of you may have seen samurai films with each warrior sitting in front of his own little table, separate from the others. I suppose it was almost like a form of meditation – eating silently. In contrast, if you've ever visited a Japanese bar or pub, where customers are

busy eating a variety of dishes (otsumami) with their drinks, you'll have noticed that silence is definitely not on the menu. In fact you'll have noticed how busy it is, with everyone rushing around and customers chatting noisily.

Japanese eating habits then are changing – as are the habits of people all around the world. We are no longer closed off to influences from the rest of the world – in fact I think that we are embracing different cuisines, ingredients and flavors with great enthusiasm. The recipes in this book reflect that experience. However, I think that even when we adopt another country's taste we subtly alter it to suit our own, and in the process we are creating a new Japanese cuisine.

Nevertheless, there are three important principles in the Japanese style of eating which remain unchanged, and which I believe mark out our cuisine as different. These are variety, seasonality and presentation.

I hope that when you use the recipes in this book you will also start looking more closely at how you serve up your food, and also when to serve particular foods. Wherever possible try to eat seasonally and use visual reminders of the season with the food. In Japanese ceramics you can easily find plates with images of red maple leaves on,

reminders of autumn, but if these are not available then maybe use a leaf or something from the garden, or a plate with autumnal color running through it.

I have designed the book so you can start by choosing a particular dish, and then serving it either as a starter or as a main course. I think you will be amazed at how easy it is to do and how different the meal experience is from what you are used to. A lot of small dishes with different flavors make a very exciting way of eating. I hope you will also notice how healthy such meals are. It is generally accepted that Japanese food is healthy and this is mainly because it aims to satisfy our needs through variety rather than quantity. However, Japanese tastes are changing, and these days it's common to find desserts using dairy products. To reflect this I have included some non-traditional desserts in my book.

I hope that you will enjoy these recipes – they were all originally published in my *Suteki Recipe* magazine and proved to be very popular. I have tried to select ones that can be easily tackled outside of Japan, relying mainly on ingredients which most of you will have in your kitchen already. There are, however, a few which are more challenging, for those of you who already know Japanese cuisine.

I hope that you will enjoy trying a new way of presenting food, of eating food, and of using tableware. But most of all I hope that attention to such things will bring you the joy and satisfaction that my mother taught me through her own example. We all know that life can be difficult and hard but the challenge is in trying to live it well. I strongly believe that we can enhance our lives by taking another look at how we eat.

So take up the challenge and enjoy a meal with all your senses; Japanese food is not frightening, just exciting and delicious!

How to Use This Book

The idea of this book is to introduce Japanese contemporary home cooking to readers around the world. It is hoped that it will demystify the cuisine and encourage people who are interested to try a new style of cooking and eating.

It is not my aim to require you, the reader, to go out and hunt down lots of obscure ingredients. I have tried to select recipes, wherever possible, that can be made fairly easily wherever you are in the world. Ingredients, even vegetables, are slightly different from country to country, so I ask you to use your common sense and to read the ingredients notes, and the glossary at the back of the book.

I have included suggestions for substitution of ingredients but I would encourage you to try these recipes even if you can't find everything needed; in most cases you will be able to achieve a result which is close to the original recipe. If you have never had Japanese food before, I would recommend that you start with the easier recipes and build up confidence and knowledge of the look and flavor of this food.

Just remember the concepts I talked about in my introduction; variety, presentation and seasonality. You can even take non-Japanese dishes and create the feel of a Japanese meal with them if you remember these principles.

Nevertheless, there are certain flavors that differ from other cuisines, which require some understanding and an open mind. One of the most obvious differences is that of sweetness: it is very common to use sugar in the preparation of a savory dish. Mirin, another important ingredient, is quite sweet and frequently used. To people who do not know Japanese food, this comes as a surprise. I believe that this sweetness balances the meal – it means we do not necessarily have strong cravings for desserts or sweets. It also balances out the saltiness of the soy sauce, miso and dashi. Try the recipes with the sugar but reduce it if it is really not to your taste.

There is also quite a saltiness to Japanese food, mainly due to soy sauce. Again, try it with the full amount of soy sauce and reduce if you really want to.

Underlying many of the recipes are the flavors of dashi, mirin and soy sauce, in various combination.

Dashi is a fish stock made with kombu seaweed and dried fish flakes (katsuo bushi). It is easy to make (see page 27), if you can get the ingredients. If you cannot find them then use a light fish stock (adding a little chicken stock if you like). You can even make it by simply boiling a piece of white fish in water. Although it is light its characteristic flavor is one worth aiming for.

Mirin is harder to substitute. It is a type of sweetened alcohol and is usually used only in cooking. It adds a great mellow, soft sweetness. Some books say you can replace it with a little extra sugar but I think that it really is worth trying to track down.

Soy sauce is now quite easy to find outside of Japan; use Japanese dark soy sauce, unless the recipe specifies light soy sauce. I think it is worth trying to find a good Japanese soy sauce as it is subtly different from the Chinese brands.

Then there is the question of herbs and spices. You should be able to find quite a lot of these items in Asian supermarkets. If you can't, try the substitutions that I have suggested. There are many recipes that need sesame paste. Tahini (a Greek sesame paste) or even unsweetened peanut butter, can be used as a substitute. However, again I would urge you to spend money on Japanese sesame paste as it is made from toasted sesame seeds and is very distinctive in its rich creaminess.

In many of my recipes you will find references to granulated chicken stock and potato starch. They are both frequently used ingredients but, if you go to a Japanese food shop, you might like to buy the original Japanese items. Torigara soup powder is what you should ask for, which is Chinese granulated chicken stock (and please note that this is different from Chinese soup paste for which I suggest you substitute a mix of chicken and beef stock). The potato starch is called katakuriko.

In addition to new flavors or combinations of flavors, you will find that there are some different styles of cooking. You will notice that I am quite relaxed about the substitution of various ingredients but I do feel strongly about the way in which vegetables are prepared for these recipes. I believe that vegetables have a very different effect on a recipe depending on how they are cut. Follow the instructions for cutting and look at the photos to replicate the look.

For all the recipes you should use really sharp knives, but especially when you are cutting raw fish. You will probably need to cultivate a good fishmonger for any of the recipes using raw fish. You should also try to master using cooking chopsticks – I think you will be amazed at just how easy they make cooking, especially any dish that's made in a wok.

As I created many of my recipes for busy people, I often include cooking instructions that feature the microwave. If you do not have one, cook the ingredients in a way that you are familiar and comfortable with. I have found, like so many Japanese, that the microwave, if used judiciously, is a great aid in the kitchen.

While I like to use modern technology, I also feel it is important to use your hands for mixing; you will get a better result if you do so. You may also find it helpful to have a few small mixing bowls ready before you start cooking – many of my recipes require you to prepare marinades, sauces or mixing ingredients at an early stage of preparation.

Quite a few recipes require you to use a lid which is placed directly on top of the food while simmering. It helps to intensify the flavors of the food being cooked and stops it moving about. If you don't have a drop lid use a circle of aluminium foil instead – just make sure it fits inside the saucepan.

For measurements, I have used the following:
1 Cup = 240ml
1 Tablespoon = 15ml
1 Teaspoon = 5ml

Finally, remember the importance of variety, presentation and seasonality when deciding which recipes to cook. Endeavor to find a balance between the flavors of the different dishes. Above all, relax and enjoy the journey into the exciting world of Japanese cuisine.

Dashi
(Fish Stock)

At the heart of many Japanese dishes is a fish-based stock called dashi. In Japan many people use instant dashi but I find this too salty and much prefer to make my own. You can subtly alter the flavor by the length of time you boil it. If you can get the ingredients it is really worth experimenting with. Good dashi can provide you with the most fantastic base, one that can transform a recipe from being just good to being fantastic.

Ingredients for 3½ cups dashi:
4¼ cups water
4-inch square piece of dried kombu seaweed
2 tablespoons dried fish flakes (katsuo bushi –
    shavings from a piece of dried bonito/tuna fish)

1 Wipe a piece of kombu seaweed with a damp cloth and then soak it in a pan with the 4¼ cups of water. I usually leave the kombu seaweed for 10 minutes.

2 Heat the water and when it is getting warm take out the piece of kombu seaweed. As the water comes to the boil add the fish flakes and cook for one or two minutes on a high heat, then turn it off. It is ready to be strained when the flakes have sunk to the bottom of the pan. These flakes are sometimes reused for a weaker version of dashi. You can freeze any unused dashi stock.

Appetizers & Entrées

When you order a drink in a bar in Japan you will always receive a small dish of food to accompany the drink – called otsumami, it's like tapas in Spain. In our family we like to do the same – to nibble on small dishes while we drink and chat, when we get together as a family at the end of a busy working day to catch up with each other's news.

Everyone in my family enjoys cooking, so we all take part in preparing a wide range of starters for us to nibble on while drinking and chatting. Sometimes we may have up to eight different appetizers – cooked by different members of the family. We each have our specialities – my husband likes cooking western-style dishes, while my daughter prefers experimenting with ethnic and Italian. My son, on the other hand, is a traditionalist and likes to cook Japanese dishes. In any case we always enjoy the relaxed informal atmosphere and having time to eat appetizers in an unhurried way.

Many of these dishes can be served as appetizers to accompany drinks or as part of a main meal as an entrée – it is up to you to decide how you want serve them.

Scallop Sauté with Miso Sauce

Hotate no Sauté Miso Sauce

These scallops make a good starter or they can be served as part of a larger Japanese-style meal. I think that the combination of Japanese flavors, such as miso, and the western flavor of Parmesan cheese makes for a delicious and exciting dish.

(Serves 4)
8 oz. very fresh scallops (without their coral)
salt and pepper
1 clove garlic, crushed
all-purpose flour – to dust the scallops
1–2 tablespoons sunflower or vegetable oil
2 tablespoons white wine
2 tablespoons miso
1 tablespoon mirin
1 teaspoon soy sauce
1 teaspoon superfine sugar (see note)
1–2 tablespoons water
½ tablespoon whole-grain mustard
2 tablespoons heavy cream
small bunch of watercress
freshly grated Parmesan cheese to taste

Ingredients Note:
Superfine sugar is a very fine granulated sugar that dissolves quickly. It is used in baking, beverages and sauces, and is available in the baking sections of supermarkets. Regular sugar can be used instead.

1 Season the scallops with the salt, pepper and garlic and then lightly dust with flour.

2 Heat the oil in a small frying pan. Briefly fry both sides of the scallops until seared on the outside, but still rare in the middle.

3 Take the pan off the heat and remove the scallops. Add the white wine and then the miso, mirin, soy sauce, sugar and water to the pan and stir. Return to the heat and bring to the boil, stirring, then remove. Mix in the mustard and heavy cream.

4 Tear the leaves off the watercress and arrange on a large plate. Chop the stems finely and set aside as a garnish. Place the scallops on the bed of watercress leaves, pour the hot sauce over and garnish with the finely chopped watercress stems. Sprinkle with Parmesan cheese and serve.

White Fish Salad

This makes a great starter or a light lunch. I like using a firm white fish like sea bream for this recipe (you could use cod or haddock).

(Serves 4)
4-6 oz. sashimi-quality white fish fillets
salt and pepper
a little crushed garlic – to taste
½ tablespoon sunflower or vegetable oil
about 5 oz. salad greens

Sesame Dressing:
3 tablespoons sesame paste
2 tablespoons hot water
a little granulated chicken stock powder
1 tablespoon superfine sugar
1 tablespoon soy sauce
1 tablespoon rice vinegar
½ tablespoon mirin
½ teaspoon red chili paste or to-ban-jan
2 tablespoons coarsely ground sesame seeds

a little finely chopped green onion or chives –
    to garnish
some coarsely ground black pepper

Ingredients Note:
If you cannot find good-quality Japanese sesame paste then use tahini (Greek sesame paste) or even unsweetened peanut butter. The final dressing should be moderately thick.

1 Season the fish with salt, pepper and garlic. In a frying pan heat the oil to medium and pan-fry both sides of the fish until it is lightly cooked but crispy on the outside. Let the fish cool and then slice diagonally into bite-size pieces.

2 Tear the salad greens, wash and drain.

3 Mix the ingredients for the sesame dressing, mixing in the order listed above but without the sesame seeds. When combined, mix in the sesame seeds.

4 Arrange the salad greens on a plate, place the sliced fish fillet on top and dress with the sesame sauce. Garnish with the chopped green onion and freshly ground black pepper.

Steamed Asari Clams with Ponzu Soy Sauce

I suppose that this recipe is Japan's answer to the famous French recipe for mussels in a white wine sauce. There is something very special about being presented with a bowl of steaming hot clams, still in their shells, and the citric fragrance from the ponzu soy sauce (see page 81) makes it a truly memorable experience.

(Serves 4)
about 1 lb. asari (manila) clams (still in their shell)
¾ cup ponzu soy sauce (see page 80)
roughly chopped shiso leaves or a mix
    of fresh mint and basil to garnish
toasted white sesame seeds to taste

1 To clean the clams, leave in salt water overnight; the water should be of the same saltiness as seawater; they will open their shells allowing the beards and sand to be removed easily. Take out any dead clams, wash well and then rub the shells together. Drain well.

2 Put a wok over medium heat. Add the clams and the ponzu soy sauce, cover with a lid and let the clams steam. When the shells open, pour the clams and sauce into a serving bowl.
Sprinkle with shiso leaves and the toasted sesame seeds.
Eat while hot.

Soy Egg Appetizers
Shoyu Tamago no Zensai

I love appetizers and party food. As well as enjoying choosing the tastes and colors of the food itself, I take great delight in deciding on which plates to display it. These eggs are just so simple to prepare but stunning to look at, with different colored toppings. You can experiment with other ideas, such as pickles, olives and cress. I happen to love any kind of egg cooking, but this is one of my favorites.

(Serves 4)
6–8 small hard-cooked eggs
1 tablespoon rice vinegar
2 tablespoons soy sauce
1 teaspoon superfine sugar

Suggested Toppings:
salmon roe
cream cheese
olives
cress
pickles

1   Shell the eggs. Mix the vinegar, soy sauce and sugar together, making sure the sugar dissolves. Put the eggs with the marinade into a large plastic bag. Leave to marinate for 2–3 hours, moving the eggs around in the bag from time to time to ensure an even color.

2   Remove the eggs from the bag and cut them in half lengthwise. Place on a serving dish and decorate the yolk with a teaspoon of salmon roe, cream cheese or any other topping you choose. Serve as finger food or with salad greens as a starter.

Chinese-Style Dumplings
Gyoza

These are often served alongside Chinese-style noodles (Ramen, see page 46) but I think they are also great for parties, barbecues or buffet meals. You can find many different recipes for dumplings but this is one of the easiest.

3 dumplings per person (Serves 4)
8 oz. uncooked shrimp
4 oz. ground pork
1 tablespoon sake
½ teaspoon salt
a pinch of sugar and pepper
1 teaspoon finely chopped ginger
2 tablespoons liquid chicken stock
1 teaspoon potato starch or cornstarch
2 oz. Chinese chives (Nira), finely chopped
2 tablespoons sesame oil
12 thin round pastry skins (you can find these
    in most Chinese supermarkets)
1½ tablespoons sunflower or vegetable oil
⅓ cup hot water
For the dipping sauce: rice vinegar and
    soy sauce with a few drops of chili oil (La-Yu)

Ingredients Note:
You should be able to find the more unusual ingredients for this recipe in Chinese supermarkets. If you can't find nira, use finely chopped green onion and 1 large clove garlic, finely chopped. Also note that the pastry skins used here are round, not rectangular.

1 First devein the shrimp by bending and, using a toothpick, pull out the dark vein. Then, with a knife, mince half of the shrimp finely and cut the rest into larger ½-inch square pieces.

2 Put the shrimp and ground pork into a large bowl and mix well. Add the sake, salt, sugar, pepper, grated ginger and stock and mix together, finally adding the starch bit by bit until you have a fairly firm paste.

3 Add the Chinese chives and half the sesame oil – this will give the mixture an appealing nutty aroma and taste.

4 Divide the mixture into 12 and shape each portion into a short sausage shape. Put each "sausage" into the center of each pastry skin and fold over.

5 Pour the sunflower oil into a large frying pan and place on a medium heat. Arrange the dumplings in rows and fry until crispy and brown on one side.

6 Turn them over and cook for a short time and then throw in the hot water, covering with a lid as quickly as you can to keep the steam in. Leave them to steam until cooked (about 5 minutes).

7 When most of the liquid is gone, uncover, pour the remaining tablespoon of sesame oil on top, and cook until crispy again. If you have a problem with the dumplings sticking to the bottom of the pan, then try wiping the bottom of the pan underneath with a damp cloth; they should come loose. Serve immediately, with a dipping sauce of vinegar, soy sauce, and chili oil – delicious!

Tuna Tartare

I got the inspiration for this recipe from a restaurant in New York. Enjoy the marriage of Japanese taste and western presentation.

(Serves 4)
1 tablespoon dashi stock or fish stock
1 tablespoon light soy sauce
1 tablespoon olive oil
½ tablespoon rice vinegar (or you can
   use lemon juice or wine vinegar instead)
a little mustard
8 oz. fresh sashimi-quality tuna
4 shiso leaves or a mix of fresh mint and basil
wasabi – to taste
1 tablespoon chopped green onions or chives
grated ginger to taste
1 tablespoon finely chopped onion
a little finely chopped garlic
a little coarsely ground pepper

1 Mix together the dashi, soy sauce, olive oil, vinegar and mustard in a bowl and set aside to use as a dressing.

2 Finely chop the tuna and shred the shiso leaves.

3 Divide the chopped tuna into three and mix one part with shiso leaves, another with the green onions or chives and the third with the finely chopped onion and garlic.

4 Make 4 tuna balls out of each bowl of tuna mix. Dress the shiso leaf-flavored balls with a dab of wasabi. Dress the green onion-flavored ones with a dab of grated ginger, and the onion and garlic balls with freshly ground pepper.

5 Serve one ball of each flavor and pour over the dressing just before eating.

Asparagus with Crab Mayonnaise Dressing

Asparagus and crab are both very popular ingredients in Japan. We mainly use the white meat from the long-legged Alaskan crab but try this with whatever crab is local to you. I like my asparagus only just cooked – so it still has a bite to it. Try it this way and you will find it is so much tastier and more satisfying than when it's soft.

(Serves 4)
1 lb. fresh green asparagus
6 oz. white crab meat
1 tablespoon white wine
½ cup mayonnaise
salt and pepper

1   Prepare the asparagus by discarding the woody ends and side leaves then boil until just cooked (about 3–5 minutes depending on thickness). Be careful not to allow the tips to become overcooked. Remove and cool by placing the asparagus into a bowl of iced water.

2   Roughly flake the crabmeat into a medium-size bowl. Sprinkle with the white wine and then mix in the mayonnaise, salt and pepper. If the dressing seems a bit stiff add a little milk; you need a soft, runny consistency.

3   Drain the asparagus and pat dry. Cut it into smaller lengths, suitable for the size of the plates you are planning to use. If there are any small pieces of asparagus that you are not putting on the plate then chop them finely and add them to the sauce. Arrange the asparagus on four individual plates and pour the crab mayonnaise over.

Soup & Noodles

We love soup! A Japanese meal needs soup – served and enjoyed at the same time as everything else. I find the western tradition of having soup at the beginning leaves me too full to enjoy the rest of the meal.

The most typical Japanese soup is misoshiru (miso soup – made with miso paste). Traditionally, it was served at every meal, but especially with breakfast. These days, although many families no longer eat a traditional breakfast, they often have miso soup with their lunch or dinner.

Miso soup is one of the best examples of how Japanese food changes according to the seasons. Although the basic soup doesn't change, the vegetables which it contains reflect the season – for example bamboo shoots in spring, aubergines in summer, mushrooms in autumn and sweet potato in winter. Soup is one of the best ways in Japanese cuisine where a large variety of seasonal ingredients can be enjoyed as a natural part of the diet.

After the Second World War, the American influence brought with it the fashion for thicker chowder and cream soups, and even now I think Japan is one of the few places outside America where you can easily find cream of corn soup. More recently however, Asian tastes like Hot and Sour Soup are gaining popularity, especially with young Japanese, like my daughter, who love the spicier foods of Southeast Asia.

There are many indigenous noodles in Japan; soba, somen and udon to name a few. We enjoy eating these noodles hot or cold, often with quite noisy gusto. But we have also adopted noodles from around the world, in particular pasta. I believe that our experience with the delicate Japanese noodles has enabled us to cook pasta in the correct al dente way. You won't find soggy pasta in any of the many Italian restaurants in Japan! What you will find is that many of these restaurants have adapted pasta to the Japanese taste, serving it with ingredients, like shiitake mushrooms and nori, not used in its native Italy.

Seafood Miso Soup

Clams are very popular in Japan, especially these small asari clams. I think they make a fantastic addition to this simple miso soup. You can make the soup even tastier by using seasonal flavors such as the leaves of the sansho plant (kinome) in spring, ginger in the summer and yuzu (a Japanese citrus fruit) in autumn and winter. It is not always easy to find kinome leaves outside Japan but use them if you can. They have a taste that makes me feel glad to have been born in Japan. If you can't find them, then experiment with chives, green onions, flat-leaf parsley or cilantro.

In this recipe I suggest using the heads of uncooked shrimp as a garnish – they look stunning and add extra taste – but don't waste the rest of the shrimp. Use them for one of the many recipes in this book that uses shrimp, like the Chinese dumpling recipe (Gyoza, see page 36).

(Serves 4)

12 oz. asari clams (or any other type of baby clam still in its shell)
1 oz. wakame seaweed
2-3 bok choy
3½ cups water
1 chicken stock cube or 2 teaspoons granulated chicken stock powder
4 uncooked shrimp heads
2 tablespoons miso
herbs such as kinome to taste

Ingredients Note:
Seaweed is really good for you and increasingly available in large supermarkets. However, if you cannot find any then try a little spinach instead.

1 Clean the clams and leave them in salted water overnight; the salted water should be similar to seawater in saltiness. When you are ready to make the soup, rinse the clams and leave them to soak for a while in unsalted water so they are ready for cooking.

2 Soak the wakame seaweed in water to remove salt, drain, squeeze and cut into bite-size pieces. Chop the bok choy into 1-inch pieces and roughly chop up the herbs.

3 Put the water in a pan and bring to the boil. Add the stock cube and let it dissolve. Then add the asari clams and the shrimp heads.

4 When the clams open (this should only take a few minutes), add the miso, wakame seaweed and bok choy. Bring it all back to the boil for a short time to ensure the miso dissolves before turning off the heat.

5 Divide among 4 bowls, ensuring that each serving contains a shrimp head. Sprinkle with the chopped herbs.

Spinach Noodle Soup

Horenso to Harusame Soup

These thin, light harusame noodles work really well in soups but if you cannot find them then try the thin Thai-style rice noodles instead. In keeping with the transparent nature of the noodles, I like to try to keep this soup looking as clear as possible by using ingredients which will not discolor the soup. Try to use white pepper and light soy sauce as it all helps to keep this looking good.

(Serves 4)
1 oz. uncooked harusame noodles
    or thin rice noodles
10 oz. fresh spinach
3½ cups water
1 tablespoon granulated chicken stock
    or 1½ chicken stock cubes
1 tablespoon sake
salt and white pepper to taste
light soy sauce to taste
1 tablespoon sesame oil
chili oil or la yu to taste

Ingredients Note:
We often use a strongly-flavored chili oil called la yu – a couple of drops in this soup will work magic.

1   In a large pan of boiling water, boil the noodles, taking care not to overcook them. Drain and then cut them into easy-to-eat lengths.

2   Briefly boil the spinach and then soak in chilled water – this helps to keep its color. Drain well and chop roughly into 1-inch lengths.

3   Bring the 3½ cups water to the boil and add the stock and sake, then the noodles and spinach. Season with salt, white pepper and light soy sauce and finally the sesame oil, which will give it an enticing aroma.

4   Chili oil can be added when the soup is served in bowls.

Egg Drop Soup
Kaki Tamago Jiru

This soup looks beautiful with its delicate yellow ribbons of egg and green herbs. It should be served and eaten while it is still very hot.

(Serves 4)
just under 4 cups dashi stock or fish stock
1 tablespoon mirin
1 tablespoon light soy sauce
½ tablespoon soy sauce
2 teaspoons water mixed with 1 teaspoon potato
   starch or cornstarch
2 eggs
chopped fresh green herbs such as mitsuba
   or green onions or even lightly cooked
   green beans
salt

Ingredients Note:
As this is a consommé-type soup it is worth trying to find the ingredients to make the dashi from scratch, as it will provide a more delicate flavor than just purchased fish stock. If you do buy the stock it may be rather salty so be careful when seasoning.

1 Warm the dashi or fish stock in a pan. Once it has come to the boil, add the mirin and soy sauces then gently thicken with the potato starch.

2 In a separate bowl lightly beat the eggs and add to the heated stock. Simmer for a few minutes, making sure not to overcook the eggs. Turn off the heat, pour into individual bowls, dress with herbs or green beans and serve immediately.

Chinese-Style Soup Noodles
Ramen

Originating in China, ramen is a Chinese soup noodle dish which we have taken and fully adapted to our taste. Once you have the basic stock and noodles you can add a variety of toppings. We have many ramen restaurants – some are so small they only have a counter big enough for 6 people to sit at. Ramen is a favorite meal for busy office workers and impoverished students as it is quick, cheap and filling. Once you have finished the noodles and the other solid ingredients, don't be afraid to pick up the bowl and drink the remaining soup – it's not considered rude. You can even make slurping noises while eating the noodles and again it is not thought of as bad mannered!

(Serves 4)
4¼ cups water
4 tablespoons granulated chicken stock
    or 6 stock cubes
½ cup pork stock (see recipe page 47)
4 tablespoons soy sauce
2 teaspoons kombu cha powder
salt to taste
20 oz. thin Chinese egg noodles – uncooked
chopped green onions to taste
menma bamboo shoots to taste
    (see Ingredients Note)
sliced simmered pork and hard-cooked eggs –
    optional (see opposite)
coarsely ground black pepper
red chili shochu – optional

Ingredients Note:
It is worth making your own pork stock for this by simmering pork as it adds real depth of flavor. If any of you are film buffs you might recall in the Japanese film *Tampopo* the search for the perfect soup for ramen. If you haven't seen the film it is worth tracking down – it will give you great insight into the making of ramen. If you cannot find kombu cha powder it can be omitted. Menma are preserved bamboo shoots that are used a lot in Chinese dishes.

1 In a large pan bring the water to a boil and add the chicken stock, pork stock, soy sauce, kombu cha powder and salt. Bring to the boil again then turn the heat down to the lowest possible heat and prepare the noodles.

2 In a separate pan bring a large quantity of water to the boil and add the noodles. Cook until *al dente*, then drain.

3 Divide the noodles among four large warmed bowls and ladle in the soup. Sprinkle some chopped green onion and the menma on top along with some sliced pork (if using). Add pepper and chili shochu, to taste.

Presentation Note:
Ramen is considered almost a complete meal, so it's usually served up in large, deep bowls – big enough to hold 2 cups of liquid per person. However, if you do not have bowls big enough then you'll have to serve smaller amounts in regular soup bowls. As an accompaniment we often serve gyoza, another Chinese import, alongside these noodles. (see page 36)

Simmered Pork

Not only does this give us a wonderful pork stock but you can use the pork and eggs on top of the ramen. Move the pork and eggs around from time to time to give them an even color.

(Serves 4)
a little sunflower or vegetable oil
1 lb. pork loin
the green part of 1 green onion
1-inch piece ginger, peeled and crushed
½ cup soy sauce
¼ cup sake
1 tablespoon superfine sugar
water
4 hard-cooked eggs (shelled)

1 Heat the oil in a saucepan to a medium heat, add the pork and sear evenly on all sides.

2 Wipe off any excess oil from the pan (you can do this with paper towels – try holding some with cooking chopsticks). Add the green onion, ginger, soy sauce, sake and sugar. Pour in enough water to almost cover the pork and increase the heat. Once it comes to the boil, turn the heat down to medium, skim the surface to remove any scum and simmer for 40 minutes. During this time turn the pork a couple of times and keep removing any scum.

3 When the water has reduced by half, add the eggs to the pan with the pork. Move them around from time to time to ensure an even color.

4 When the water has reduced to about ½ cup, turn off the heat and leave to cool, then slice the pork and cut the eggs in half. Use the stock to make the ramen and put the meat and eggs on top.

Sesame Miso Soup with Tofu

Although young Japanese increasingly begin the day by eating a western-style breakfast, it is hard to imagine my parents serving anything other than a traditional one, which always includes homemade miso soup. This sesame soup recipe is a tasty variation on that theme. Miso and sesame are a very good combination and you don't need many ingredients to make this rich and delicious soup. I quite often use ready-made sesame paste but my mother prefers to stick to the traditional way and grinds her own paste from toasted sesame seeds. The aroma from the soup is amazing and drinking it seems to make your sleepiness disappear, waking you up and giving you strength for the day ahead.

1 If you are not using sesame paste, start by roasting the sesame seeds. Be careful not to burn the seeds, taking the pan off the heat once the seeds start to pop.

2 In a pestle and mortar, grind them to a sticky paste. It should smell wonderfully nutty as the seeds give off their aroma. Transfer the paste into a large mixing bowl.

3 Pour the dashi or fish stock into a pan over a moderate heat. Just before it comes to the boil add the miso paste, stirring until it dissolves. Bring to a gentle boil, slowly mix in the sesame paste and add the tofu, breaking it up into bite-size pieces with your hands.

4 Serve immediately, garnished with a little chopped green onion and a little ground sesame according to taste. You can also add seasonal cooked vegetables if you like.

(Serves 4)
½ cup sesame seeds or 4–5 tablespoons
   sesame paste
3½ cups dashi or fish stock
1 (12.3-oz.) box soft silken tofu
4 tablespoons miso paste

Ingredients Note:
I prefer to use the soft silken tofu here but you can use the firm type if you prefer. The idea of breaking the tofu into small pieces with your hands comes from a Chinese style of Buddhist vegetarian cooking called Hucha Ryori. In Japan we have a traditional style of vegetarian cooking called Shojin Ryori – again based on Buddhist principles.

Pan-Fried Noodles with Pork and Bok Choy
Yakisoba

This meal is ideal when you have only one package of Chinese noodles left. You can substitute beef, chicken or any ground meat for the pork and it still tastes great. Just make sure that it is served up as quickly as possible – noodles should always be eaten piping hot. This is also a great recipe to try using cooking chopsticks, which are longer than the ones used to eat with. They are an essential part of any Japanese cook's equipment, and are particularly useful for quick stir-frying.

(Serves 2)
2 inches fresh ginger (peeled)
2-3 bok choy
4 oz. pork (most cuts will do)
salt and pepper
1½ cups hot water
1 teaspoon Chinese soup paste or a mix
   of chicken and beef stock
1 tablespoon soy sauce
1 tablespoon shokoshu
1 teaspoon oyster sauce
2 tablespoons sunflower or vegetable oil
5-6 oz. cooked Chinese noodles
1½ tablespoons potato starch mixed
   with 1½ tablespoons water
1 tablespoon sesame oil
rice vinegar and mustard

1 Crush the ginger using the blade of a knife. Chop the bok choy stems into 2-inch juliennes and keep separate. Season the pork with salt and pepper and cut it into small strips.

2 Mix the hot water, soup paste/stock, soy sauce, shokoshu and oyster sauce in a bowl to use as a sauce later.

3 Heat 1 tablespoon of the sunflower oil in a wok over a medium heat. Loosen the Chinese noodles, add to the frying pan, pressing them into the bottom. When they are crispy, turn them over and cook on the other side. This is done to make them crunchy. Separate them again and then put them on a warm plate.

4 Pour a little more oil into the wok, add the ginger and fry. When you can smell its aroma, then add the pork and press it down.

5 Next, add the bok choy stems and after 1 minute add the leaves. Stir in the sauce you made earlier.

6 Bring to a simmer and add the potato starch, thickening to taste. Add the sesame oil for an extra special aroma.

7 Remove the piece of ginger and pour the sauce over the noodles. Add vinegar and Japanese mustard to taste.

Japanese Somen Noodle Salad

When I asked my husband which of my recipes he liked the best, he immediately answered, "Somen salad!" You can cook this simple dish using ingredients that you probably already have in your cupboard. If you do not have these noodles you can use something else like spaghettini. It is a very versatile salad that can be used to accompany many meals – it also works well in lunchboxes.

(Serves 2–3)
3½ oz. somen noodles
3 oz. canned tuna (or ham, if you prefer)
½ small onion
½ small to medium cucumber
4 tablespoons mayonnaise
a little salt, pepper and soy sauce

Ingredients Note:
Cucumbers in Japan are small – which means they are less watery than large ones. Try to get small cucumbers, but if you can't then use a large one and scoop out the seeds from the middle.

1 Fill a large pan with plenty of water and bring to the boil. Add the noodles to the pan and cook until *al dente*. When cooked, rinse under cold running water, ensuring that the noodles are all separated, then drain well.
2 Drain the tuna. Cut the onion thinly into half moons and soak in water for about 5–10 minutes to take away any sharpness. Drain the onion and squeeze to remove any excess water. Finely slice the cucumber and season with salt. Leave for 5–10 minutes then squeeze to remove any excess water.
3 Mix the noodles, tuna, onion, cucumber and mayonnaise in a bowl and season with salt, pepper and soy sauce.

Spaghettini with Fish Roe Dressing
Mentaiko Spaghettini

This is one of the most popular types of pasta in Japan and is a great example of how a foreign ingredient has been adapted to Japanese taste. I think you will find it quite an eye opener.

(Serves 2)
6 oz. uncooked spaghettini
3 oz. mentaiko (see Ingredients Note)
2 tablespoons butter
nori seaweed to taste
shiso leaves or fresh basil and mint leaves to taste
½ teaspoon kombu cha powder
soy sauce to season
chopped green onion or chives to garnish

Ingredients Note:
Mentaiko is quite difficult to substitute. Its unique taste comes from the salting process and chili. Kombu cha powder may also be hard to substitute, but you can make something similar with a little strong fish stock.

1 Boil the spaghettini in a pan of salted water until *al dente*.
2 Soften the butter and beat until creamy. Remove the thin membrane from the mentaiko and mix the roe with the butter.
3 Finely shred the dried seaweed and the shiso leaves.
4 When the spaghettini is cooked, drain well. Immediately mix with the mentaiko and the butter and season with kombu cha powder and soy sauce.
5 Put onto a serving plate, sprinkle the dried seaweed and shiso leaves on top and garnish with green onions or chives.

Rice

I cannot live without rice, and I think many Japanese people feel the same. Like other Asians we just love rice. In fact I could eat rice three times a day, but I certainly have to have it at least once a day. The rice we use in Japan is short grained, which becomes sticky when cooked – this makes it easier to eat with chopsticks. We never use the long-grain "fluffy" rice. At the risk of sounding a little nationalistic I think that Japanese rice is the best in the world.

As it is such an important element in a Japanese meal it is worth trying different varieties to find the one that suits you the best. I continually try rice from different regions of Japan as different regions produce rice of a subtly different flavor or texture. I find that one particular type will complement a particular meal better than another. Some people like rice which can be described as watery but personally I prefer a firmer variety of rice. I also think that the best rice is rice which is harvested in the autumn.

Ideally rice should be eaten plain – in other words without covering it in sauces or frying it with other ingredients. That way you can really appreciate the subtle flavor of the grain itself, and once you've learned to recognize it you'll be appalled at the sight of people pouring gallons of soy sauce onto their rice.

In our house we use probably at least twice as much rice as other traditional households – mainly because we have so many visitors. Most people these days have electric rice cookers, and many of them use the cooker to cook rice overnight so it's ready for the next morning, but I don't advocate this myself. I think that rice needs to be treated with respect and should be freshly prepared for each meal.

In fact, one of the main reasons I get up so early is to prepare rice, which we then have for breakfast, and to make lunchboxes for the family. My son loves onigiri (rice balls) in his lunchbox because, like sandwiches, they are easy to pick up and eat, and with a variety of fillings they are also very tasty. In fact nearly all traditional lunch-boxes (called bento) will include rice, and, even though it's eaten cold, it's still delicious. For added flavor we sometimes sprinkle sesame seeds on top or place a pink umeboshi (pickled plum) in the center – which looks pretty as well as tasting good.

Preparation for Rice Cooking

Traditionally, Japanese rice needs to be washed extensively before cooking. This has changed recently with the introduction of "musenmai" – rice that has already been washed. However, it is still difficult to find this pre-washed rice outside Japan, so I would like to explain how to wash Japanese rice.

My mother was really fussy about how the rice was washed and many women of her generation have tried and tested methods of cleaning the rice. I think the best way is to put the rice into a bowl of water and, using your hands, swill it around and then drain into a sieve. You will see that the water is a very milky color – the rice needs to be washed until the water turns clear. You need to scoop the rice up through the water and then lightly press it down with the heel of your hands. Repeat this action around 20 times, drain, add more water and repeat until the water clears. It creates quite a rhythmic sound as the rice swishes around in the water.

On average, I think it should take around 2–3 minutes to complete the washing. Once the water is clear, drain it and leave it for 30 minutes before cooking. During this time the rice should visibly plump up.

Most Japanese households these days have electric rice cookers, which are very convenient and easy to use. If you have a rice cooker then use it.

Cooking Rice in a Saucepan

Take a heavy-bottomed saucepan and put in the rice and the cold water. You should use slightly more water than rice and no salt. Bring to the boil – when you hear it boil, put on a tight-fitting lid and turn the heat down low and cook for a further 15 minutes. Turn off the heat and leave for a further 10 minutes. Do not take the lid off at any time during the cooking. After it has rested, take off the lid and stir the rice. To do this, you need to cut through the rice with a wooden spoon and turn the rice from the bottom to the top. Don't try to break up the rice too much, the idea is to stop it being one solid mass but not separate the grains as with long-grain rice.

If you cook your rice like this, it should be perfect – sticky but with a slight bite. If you have never had Japanese rice before, you will perhaps be surprised by the way it sticks together – do not worry as this is correct for this type of rice; it makes it easier to eat with chopsticks. If you find you have cooked too much you can always freeze anything left over or use it in a lunchbox. Japanese rice is really tasty, even cold.

How Much Rice?

As I mentioned in the introduction, I eat a lot of rice but I suggest that you use around 2 cups of uncooked rice with 2½ cups water for around 4 people. As a rough rule of thumb, 1 cup of uncooked rice makes 1½ to 2 cups cooked rice. Each household will be different, so you might need to adjust according to your own taste.

Beef on Rice
Gyudon

As you will have noticed in this section there are a number of recipes where something is served on top of a bowl of rice. It is such an easy and quick way to eat, especially at lunchtime. This recipe features a richly flavored beef and onion topping. The combination of beef and onions gives it a sweet but spicy taste. You can use almost any type of beef, as the wine tenderizes it.

(Serves 4)
1 lb. onions
1 cup white wine
½ cup water
1 lb. thinly sliced beef
¾ cup soy sauce
¾ cup mirin
4 tablespoons superfine sugar
3 cups hot cooked rice
pickled ginger (beni shoga) to taste

1 Cut the onions in half lengthwise and then slice into half moons ½ inch wide.

2 In a medium-size saucepan, bring the wine and water to the boil over moderate heat. Add the beef and simmer for a few minutes, skimming the surface of the broth as it foams. Add the soy sauce, mirin and sugar and cover with a drop lid of aluminium foil (see cooking note) and simmer for a few more minutes.

3 Remove the lid, add the onions and again simmer until the onions are transparent and soft.

4 Put the hot cooked rice into 4 bowls. Ladle the beef and onions, together with some soup from the pan onto each rice bowl and garnish with a little pickled red ginger.

Cooking Note:
In this recipe we use a drop lid (called an otoshi buta) which is a wooden lid which drops inside a saucepan and sits directly on top of the food. We use this cooking technique frequently as it reduces the amount of liquid needed for cooking and concentrates the flavor. These days, even in Japan, many people use a circle of aluminium foil instead of a wooden lid – the important thing is that this "lid" rests on top of the food, in the pan.

Three Types of Mixed Rice
Maze Gohan

Rice is a wonderful ingredient to work with. I like taking cooked rice and mixing it with a variety of different flavors. I have created these dressings with deliberately light flavors so they work well with both hot and cold rice. They can be used either on top of the rice or mixed into the rice and served as rice balls. Also, they can be made in advance and are useful to serve with many different dishes. Each recipe is for 4–5 servings and the photos below show all three dressings.

Mixed Mushrooms Dressing:
4 oz. fresh shiitake mushrooms
3 oz. maitake mushrooms
3 oz. shimeji mushrooms
3 tablespoons soy sauce
2 tablespoons mirin
½ teaspoon dried fish flakes (optional)
2 tablespoons white sesame seeds

Ingredients Note:
If you cannot get these Japanese mushrooms then use a mixture of whatever fresh mushrooms you can obtain.

1 Remove the stems from all the mushrooms and wipe clean. Cut the shiitake mushrooms into 4 pieces. Divide the maitake and shimeji mushrooms into small bunches.
2 Put the soy sauce and mirin into a small pan and bring to the boil. Add all the mushrooms to the pan and cook over moderate heat until the liquid has been absorbed. Add the dried fish flakes and toss all the ingredients together. Sprinkle the sesame seeds on top.

Salmon Dressing:
8 oz. salmon
2 tablespoons sake
2 teaspoons mirin
1 teaspoon salt
a little light soy sauce

1 Place the salmon on a microwave-safe plate and sprinkle the sake on top. Cover with a lid and microwave on medium for 2½ minutes. Leave to cool.

2 Discard any bones or skin from the salmon and then roughly flake the flesh.

3 Put the cooked salmon in a pan with the mirin and salt and cook for a few minutes over medium heat. Finally, season with the light soy sauce. If you are serving this as rice balls place a little salmon roe on top to add color – and taste.

Spicy Clam Dressing:
About 5 oz. canned clams or baby clams
2-inch piece of peeled ginger
1 tablespoon sake
1 tablespoon superfine sugar
3 tablespoons soy sauce
2 tablespoons mirin

1 Drain the clams.

2 Cut the ginger into fine juliennes.

3 Put the clams and the sake into a small pan and cook over moderate heat for a few minutes. Add the sugar, soy sauce and mirin. Finally, add the ginger and cook until the liquid has been absorbed.

Cooking Note:
Microwave ovens usually range from 800 to 1,200 watts; they cook foods at different rates. For these recipes, it is assumed the microwave has about 1,000 watts. If yours is more or less adjust cooking time accordingly.

Japanese-Style Green Risotto
Aona Zosui

This simple Japanese-style risotto makes an excellent breakfast on cold mornings or it can be served as a light meal during the rest of the day. A Japanese breakfast often starts with rice and eggs and this recipe is very much in keeping with this tradition, but the greens add a more contemporary slant to it. I use two or three different kinds of green leaves – whatever I have in the fridge at the time.

(Serves 4)
4 eggs
¾ cup Japanese parsley (seri – similar in flavor to flat-leaf parsley)
4 oz. shungiku (chrysanthemum leaves – arugula could be a suitable substitute)
1½ cups mitsuba (a little like cilantro)
3½ cups dashi or fish stock
1 tablespoon light soy sauce
½ teaspoon salt
¾ cup cooked rice (preferably Japanese-style rice)
soy sauce to taste

1 Make Hot Spring–Style Eggs. (See page 75, Tofu with Hot Spring Eggs.)
2 Put the Japanese parsley, shungiku and mitsuba in a pan of boiling water for about 30 seconds each, then drain and soak in iced water. Squeeze the leaves lightly and chop into ½-inch length pieces. (Follow this method if you are using other green leaves – though if they are thicker than parsley they might need to be cooked a little longer.)
3 Put the dashi stock, light soy sauce and salt in a saucepan and heat. Once it has come to the boil, add the rice and turn down the heat so that it simmers gently. Stir constantly and, when it thickens, turn off the heat. Squeeze the greens again, add to the pan and mix in.
4 Divide among 4 bowls placing a hot spring egg on top of each. Season with soy sauce to taste.

Fried Rice with Octopus

Tako Chahan

Simple stir-fried dishes like this, or the stir-fried noodles in the previous section, are very popular – especially with students who will create endless versions of this dish using whatever they have on hand. The secret is to make sure it is well seasoned and served piping hot.

(Serves 4)
6 oz. cooked octopus legs
1 oz. dried shiitake mushrooms
1 green pepper
8 green onions
1 clove garlic
2 tablespoons sunflower or vegetable oil
3 cups hot cooked rice (preferably Japanese rice)
1 tablespoon oyster sauce
½ tablespoon soy sauce
salt and pepper to taste
a pinch of granulated chicken stock
1 tablespoon sesame oil

1 Slice the octopus thinly. Soak the dried shiitake mushrooms in water until rehydrated. Squeeze lightly and then roughly chop the mushrooms, green pepper and green onions. Finely mince the garlic.

2 Heat the sunflower oil in a frying pan over moderate heat. Add the chopped garlic and fry for a minute or so, until the garlic aroma is released, then add the sliced octopus and heat through. Remove to stop it getting too tough but keep it ready to add later.

3 Add the green onions, green pepper and shiitake mushrooms and fry again.

4 Stir in the hot rice, mixing well and season with oyster sauce, soy sauce, salt, pepper and granulated stock.

5 Finally mix in the octopus, season with the sesame oil and serve immediately.

Ingredients Note:
If you can't get octopus ready cooked then you'll have to prepare it yourself. Have your fishmonger cut off the body then take the legs (which you are going to eat) and sprinkle with a little salt – too much will make it chewy. Rub the legs to get rid of any stickiness and then wash thoroughly under cold running water. Boil for 2–3 minutes, drain, leave to cool and pat dry.

Garlic Fried Rice
Ninniku Chahan

This fried rice smells amazing and is so quick to do. I often serve this up as an accompaniment to steak. If you have the time, I like to shape individual portions with a small mold, using something like a ramekin dish, and then turn it out onto the plate. It is easy to do but looks so impressive!

(Serves 4)
1-2 garlic cloves
10 shiso leaves or a mix of fresh basil
    and mint leaves
2 tablespoons sunflower or vegetable oil
2 cups cooked rice – Japanese if possible
1 teaspoon granulated chicken stock
soy sauce
dried fish flakes (if available)
coarsely ground pepper

1   Finely chop the garlic and then cut the shiso leaves into ⅓-inch square pieces.

2   Heat the oil in a wok and fry the garlic, until you can smell it. Then add the rice and stock powder.

3   Add the soy sauce by pouring it onto the inside surface of the pan and mixing it in. Turn off the heat, add the shiso leaves and mix quickly, then serve either in the way I described above or on one large plate. Use the dried fish flakes and pepper as garnish.

Finely Chopped Tuna on Rice

Maguro no Tataki Don

I use tuna so frequently that I find it handy to keep some in the freezer, available for whenever I need it. For this recipe I like to chop the tuna in two different ways; half finely chopped and half roughly chopped. As you might have noticed with my recipes, I like to pay attention to how things are cut – I think this may be a rather Japanese tendency. Cutting ingredients in a variety of ways creates different textures as well as making a dish look different. Try it and see if you notice a difference.

(Serves 4)
4-6 oz. sashimi-quality raw tuna
4 green onions or shallots
1 oz. myoga (optional)
10 shiso leaves or a mix of fresh basil and mint
2 tablespoons freshly grated ginger
salmon roe to taste
a little shredded daikon (mooli or Japanese white radish)
2½ cups cooked rice – Japanese, if possible
4 egg yolks – optional
soy sauce

Ingredients Note:
There are many different cuts of raw tuna for sashimi but for this recipe I like to use medium fatty tuna, chutoro. The most highly valued tuna is the really fatty tuna, or otoro, which just melts in the mouth.

Egg Safety:
Uncooked or undercooked eggs should not be eaten by young children or the elderly, or anyone with an illness that may have weakened the immune system. Uncooked eggs may contain salmonella bacteria that can cause food poisioning and serious illness. Salmonella is destroyed by cooking.

Pasteurized eggs are available in some markets and are safe to eat uncooked. They are more expensive than regular eggs.

1 Chop half of the tuna finely, and the rest roughly.
2 Chop the green onion, myoga and shiso leaves roughly.
3 Then put the tuna, vegetables, grated ginger and salmon roe in a bowl and mix lightly.
4 Chop the daikon into thin matchsticks. Put some hot rice into four bowls and top with the daikon and then the tuna mix. I like to serve this with a raw egg yolk, so if you want to do this make sure the eggs are very fresh. Make a small well in the center of the tuna mix and pop in the egg yolk. Add some soy sauce to taste.

Tofu

I am sure that many people outside Asia wonder what on earth to do with tofu – it seems to be such an alien taste and texture for westerners. However, if you try the following recipes I'm sure you will find that it is a wonderful and versatile ingredient.

In Japan we used to have specialist tofu makers who, like the bakers of Europe, would get up early every morning to prepare this essential food, so it was fresh for the day ahead.

Nowadays there are not many old-style tofu makers left , and most people buy tofu from their local supermarket. Outside of Japan you can usually find it in your local health food shop or in the vegetarian section of many large supermarkets.

There are two types of tofu – soft (silken tofu or kinugoshi) and hard or firm (momengoshi). The texture of tofu is part of its appeal, and, as the texture of one is quite different from the other, you may find you prefer a particular style. Personally I always use the soft or silken type. The only time I use firm tofu is for frying, because it holds its shape better.

Most Japanese like tofu, and eat it in many different ways. We have it hot in soups, we include it in stews in winter and eat it cold with various dressings in summer.

In fact I think tofu is such a healthy, cheap and versatile ingredient that I hope you will come to enjoy it and use it as frequently as I do.

Tofu with Basil and Gorgonzola Dressing

This is a rather Italian way to serve up tofu but I think the strong flavors of basil and Gorgonzola work well with the mild flavor of the tofu. Despite a traditional aversion to cheese, modern Japanese are beginning to enjoy the many types available – even strong ones like Gorgonzola!

For this recipe, I think it's better to break the tofu into pieces with your hands rather than to cut it with a knife, as this ensures that the dressing coats the tofu more effectively. Purchased pesto sauce is usually too thick to use as a dressing for tofu, so this recipe thins it down with the addition of some stock.

(Serves 4)
12 oz. firm tofu
2 tablespoons pesto sauce
1 tablespoon liquid chicken stock
1 medium tomato
fresh basil leaves to garnish
ripe Gorgonzola to taste

1 Drain off the water from the tofu, wrap in paper towels and leave to drain.
2 Mix the pesto sauce with the chicken stock – adding more or less according to the thickness of the pesto sauce. The final sauce should be quite runny.
3 Chop the tomato into small pieces and tear up the basil leaves.
4 Divide the tofu into four bowls and, using half the pesto mix, pour a little over each piece of tofu. Then crumble some gorgonzola over and sprinkle with the chopped tomato and basil leaves. Finally, pour the remaining pesto mix over the top.

Fried Tofu with Bean Sprouts and Bok Choy
Tofu to Moyashi no Chingensai Itame

I have a passion for bean sprouts and recommend that you take the time to remove the tips from each sprout. It really does make a difference. The key to success with this recipe is removing excess moisture from the tofu and then cooking it in hot sesame oil.

(Serves 4)
12 oz. firm tofu
9 oz. bean sprouts
2-3 bok choy
1 tablespoon sesame oil
1 tablespoon sunflower or vegetable oil
2 teaspoons granulated chicken stock
salt and pepper
coarsely ground white sesame seeds to taste

1 Drain the tofu and then wrap in paper towels and place in a strainer for 30 minutes to remove excess water.

2 Discard the roots from the bean sprouts and wash, then drain well.

3 Cut the white stems of the bok choy lengthwise into 1–1½ inches and chop the green leaves horizontally into 1–1½-inch pieces.

4 Heat the sesame oil in a frying pan. Break up the tofu by hand and fry for a few minutes. When it is really sizzling, remove from the pan and place it on a dish.

5 Add the sunflower oil to the frying pan and heat, add the pak choy and then the bean sprouts. Return the tofu to the pan, mix with the vegetables and season with the chicken stock powder and salt and pepper.

6 Put the cooked tofu and vegetables into an attractive serving dish and sprinkle with the sesame seeds.

Deep-Fried Tofu with Japanese Dressing
Agedashi Dofu

This is a wonderful classic recipe, delicious all year round. The key is to get the tofu crispy and the correct flavor for the dressing.

(Serves 4)
2 (12.3-oz.) boxes soft silken tofu
potato starch or cornstarch for dusting
   the tofu pieces
oil – enough to deep-fry the tofu
1 cup dashi stock or fish stock
2 tablespoons mirin
2 tablespoons soy sauce
a little superfine sugar
a little salt
grated daikon (mooli or Japanese white radish)
grated ginger to taste
shiso leaves, chopped into thin strips or a mix
   of fresh basil and mint leaves
myoga, minced (optional)
green onion or chives, minced

Ingredients Note:
Daikon is a very commonly used vegetable in
Japanese cooking. This recipe does not use much
but if you can find some it adds extra flavor and
texture for this dish. It is often served in this way,
raw and grated, as an accompaniment to grilled or
fried dishes.

1 Drain the tofu and then wrap it in paper towels and place
in a strainer for 30 minutes to remove excess moisture.
2 Cut the tofu into four pieces, dry again with paper towels,
then coat with the potato starch.
3 Heat the oil to a suitable temperature for deep-frying (around
340°F). Carefully put the tofu pieces in to fry, and when they turn
golden, remove and drain on paper towels to remove excess oil.
4 In a small pan heat up the dashi stock, mirin, soy sauce, sugar
and salt. Bring to the boil, ensuring that the sugar has dissolved.
5 Divide the tofu among four bowls. Pour a little of the hot sauce
into each bowl and garnish with the grated daikon, a dab
of grated ginger, shiso, myoga and green onion to taste.

Tofu with Hot Spring Eggs (Onsen Tamago)
Onsen Tamago Nose Dofu

I think the best way to enjoy tofu is to eat it in the simplest possible way so you get to really appreciate the subtle and delicate taste of the tofu itself. Then you can add depth with tasty condiments and toppings. This particular recipe is simplicity itself and shows just how versatile and delicious tofu can be.

(Serves 4)
2 (12.3-oz.) boxes soft silken tofu
4 hot spring eggs (see following recipe and
　　Egg Safety, page 66)
1 teaspoon dried fish flakes
¼ cup soy sauce
2 tablespoons mirin
1 tablespoon sake
chopped green onions or chives to taste
grated fresh ginger to taste

How to make "Hot Spring Eggs" (onsen tamago):
　Put the eggs into a wideneck flask (or any other container that will hold heat) – make sure they are at room temperature, not chilled. Add boiling water to cover them and leave for 10 minutes. The yolk should still be runny with the white just cooked. It couldn't be easier.

　There are many hot springs in Japan – the result of the volcanic makeup of the country – and eggs are often cooked in the boiling waters of the hot spring. The eggs take on a very strong sulphuric flavor that is popular with the Japanese but not always with visitors from overseas.

1 Drain the tofu and wrap in paper towels to remove excess water.

2 Make the dressing by combining the dried fish flakes, soy sauce, mirin and sake in a microwave-safe bowl and cooking it in the microwave on medium for 2 minutes. Leave to cool and then strain. If you cannot obtain the fish flakes then use a little concentrated fish stock to give a slight fish flavor to the dressing.

3 Cut the tofu into 4 pieces and place one piece in each bowl. Scoop out a hollow in each one and put a "hot spring egg" in each hollow (see Egg Safety, page 66).

4 Arrange the scooped tofu around the edge. Scatter some green onions on top and dab on a little grated ginger.

5 Pour the dressing over the tofu and serve.

Tofu Steak

I think that tofu novices are amazed that tofu can be as good as this. Tofu in this recipe is cooked in a similar way to steak – seasoned with salt, pepper and garlic and then sizzled. It should be cooked so that the outside is crispy and the inside hot. Serve it with lots of different vegetables and eat with soy sauce and Japanese wasabi (horseradish).

(Serves 4)
2 (12.3-oz.) boxes of soft silken tofu
½ red pepper
½ yellow pepper
2 small zucchini
8 oz. fresh green asparagus
4oz. maitake mushrooms or other
  fresh mushrooms
3 small tomatoes
2 cloves garlic
4 tablespoons olive oil
a little pepper and salt
a little crushed garlic
a little all-purpose flour
soy sauce and wasabi to taste

1 Drain the tofu, wrap in paper towels and place in a strainer for 30 minutes to remove any excess water.

2 Cut the peppers lengthwise and remove the seeds. Slice into 3 lengthwise. Cut the zucchini into 1-inch rounds. Cut off woody parts of the asparagus. Roughly tear up the maitake mushrooms. Cut the tomatoes in half. Peel the garlic cloves.

3 Heat half the olive oil in a frying pan and add the whole garlic. When you can smell the garlic, add the vegetables and let them sizzle for 5 minutes. Remove and place on a warm plate.

4 Cut the tofu into four pieces and season them with salt, pepper and crushed garlic. Dust lightly with flour. Add the remaining olive oil to the frying pan and heat to a fairly high temperature. Place the tofu in the oil, then when it turns crispy on one side turn it over, then repeat on all sides. Remove when each piece is crispy and golden.

5 Serve with the cooked vegetables and a mixture of soy sauce and wasabi.

Tofu and Ground Pork Kebabs
Tofu no Tsukune

These kebabs have a slight Southeast Asian flavor to them with the addition of cilantro and Thai fish sauce. The addition of tofu helps make these kebabs a little lighter and healthier than kebabs made only with meat.

(Makes 8 kebabs)
12 oz. firm tofu
2 oz. green beans
small bunch fresh mint leaves
small bunch fresh cilantro leaves
6 oz. ground pork
¼ cup finely chopped onion

For the marinade:
2 teaspoons Thai fish sauce
1 teaspoon light soy sauce
1 teaspoon of the juice from some grated ginger
a little salt
2 tablespoons sunflower or vegetable oil
serve with sanchu, cilantro, sweet chili sauce
   and lemon juice to taste

1 Wrap the tofu in paper towels and place in a strainer for 30 minutes to remove excess water.

2 Remove ends from the green beans and boil them until they are just cooked. Drain and then soak in chilled water. When cooled, drain again and cut into ½-inch pieces.

3 Chop the mint and cilantro leaves roughly and mix.

4 Put the ground pork and the ingredients for the marinade into a bowl and mix well by hand until it becomes sticky.

5 Break the tofu into small pieces by hand and add to the pork mixture along with the beans, cilantro, mint and onion. Mix thoroughly again; I find it best to do this by hand.

6 Divide the mixture into 8 pieces and shape each one into a sausage shape. Heat the oil in a frying pan and fry the kebabs until they brown on the outside and are cooked right through.

7 If you want, put a skewer in each kebab and arrange on a plate (you can also serve these like hamburgers). Serve with some sanchu and cilantro, sweet chili sauce and lemon wedges.

Ingredients Note:
Sanchu is a type of lettuce leaf that resembles butter lettuce and is not crunchy like romaine or iceberg.

Tofu and Avocado Dressing

This beautiful pale green–colored sauce is a very useful addition to many meals. I particularly like serving it with deep-fried chicken pieces or with grilled shrimp or fish. The combination of avocado and tofu gives it a real richness and a melt-in-the-mouth texture that is quite special.

6 oz. soft silken tofu (½ box)
1 medium ripe avocado
a little lemon juice
3 tablespoons cottage cheese
1½ teaspoons granulated chicken stock
2 tablespoons mayonnaise
salt and pepper

Ingredients Note:
It is quite important with this recipe to use silken (or kinugoshidofu) tofu. If you use the firm type it will be much more difficult to achieve the necessary texture.

1. Wrap the tofu in paper towels and place on a strainer for 30 minutes to drain.
2. Peel the avocado, take out the seed and put the flesh in a mixing bowl. Add a little lemon juice and mash. Cut or break the tofu into bite-size pieces, add to the avocado and mix together with the cottage cheese. Mix well using a balloon whisk.
3. Finally, add the granulated stock, mayonnaise and salt and pepper and serve immediately.

Hot Tofu with Ponzu Soy Sauce

Tofu makes a very welcome addition to any casserole dish. The tofu takes on the flavor of the stock and becomes quite a feast – as with shabu shabu (see page 120). In this recipe the tofu is cooked in a tasty stock and then dipped into ponzu soy sauce, and it's especially comforting in winter.

(Serves 4)
3½ cups dashi stock or fish stock
2 sheets 4-inch square kombu seaweed
6-8 baby leeks or large green onions
4 oz. enoki mushrooms
chopped green onions or chives to garnish
shichimi togarashi (a mixture of red pepper
  and other spices)

Ponzu Soy Sauce:
½ cup yuzu or kabosu juice
  (see Ingredients Note)
½ cup mirin
¾ cup soy sauce
¼ cup light soy sauce
4-inch square kombu seaweed
  (wipe off any excess saltiness)

Ingredients Note:
Yuzu and kabosu are Japanese citrus fruits;
yuzu is similar to a lime and kabosu to a lemon,
so if you cannot find them then use lemons
or limes.

1 Pour the dashi stock into a casserole dish and add the kombu seaweed. Leave for 30 minutes.

2 Cut the tofu into 6 square pieces. Slice the leeks diagonally into ½-inch-wide pieces. Chop off the bottom part of the enoki mushrooms and discard.

3 Place the casserole dish over a medium heat and bring it to a boil. Turn down to a simmer and add the tofu. When it comes back to the boil again, add the leeks and mushrooms. Cook on a gentle heat until the leeks are tender. Serve with the ponzu soy sauce, chopped green onions and the shichimi togarashi.

Ponzu Soy Sauce:

1 Squeeze ½ cup of juice from the citrus fruits, making sure to remove any seeds.

2 Add the mirin to the citric juice and microwave uncovered on medium for 3 minutes and leave to cool.

3 Add the two types of soy sauce and mix well.

4 Put into a sterilized bottle with the piece of kombu seaweed. It will keep in the refrigerator for up to a month.

Seafood

I was fortunate to grow up in a village next to the sea where there was an endless supply of delicious fresh fish. My mother, like the other women of the village, knew the local fishmonger and would buy fish according to the season. These days we go to the supermarket and can find almost any type of fish all through the year, but if you can buy seasonally you will find a great improvement in flavor.

Traditionally, a basic meal in a Japanese home would consist of misoshiru (miso soup), rice, pickles and fish. Often the fish would be grilled whole and served up individually on rectangular plates. We like to see the shape of the fish and we're not afraid to eat parts of the fish, like the eyes, that many in the west find unacceptable.

We serve up fish and seafood in many ways. In the days before refrigeration we had to devise ways of preserving fish – using miso, salt, vinegar or even drying it. Like the Portuguese bacalao, even though these techniques are no longer strictly necessary for preservation, we still use them, as we enjoy the taste and the romance of them.

Nevertheless, to a Japanese person, the best way to enjoy fish and seafood is to eat it raw, as sashimi or in sushi – though it needs to be really fresh to be eaten this way. If you visit Japan it is worth visiting the fresh fish section in supermarkets and department stores or, even better, the famous Tokyo fish market, "Tsukiji" – the biggest in the world – where you can see a bewildering variety of fish, including many species which are unavailable outside Asia.

My family consumes vast quantities of fish – I think we probably are the number one consumers of fish in the area in which I live!

Salmon Burgers

I think that the Japanese are very creative in taking dishes from around the world and adapting and re-creating them to our taste. Most Japanese love fish and many also love burgers – which gave me the inspiration for the following recipe. The texture of this burger is quite different from beef burgers, which I think can be too dry. These salmon burgers are really juicy and can be served with different sauces for different tastes.

(Serves 4)
12 oz. fresh salmon
½ small onion
1 tablespoon butter
1 small potato, peeled
4 oz. ground or coarsely chopped pork
a little beaten egg
salt and pepper
sunflower or vegetable oil for frying

Soy Dressing:
3 tablespoons soy sauce
1 tablespoon lemon juice
1 teaspoon chili paste or to-ban-jan
superfine sugar to taste
a small handful of freshly chopped cilantro
　leaves to garnish

Other Suggested Toppings:
mayonnaise with coarsely ground pepper
　to taste
pesto sauce

1　Remove any bones or skin from the salmon. Chop finely until it is almost ground.

2　Chop the onion into ¼- to ⅓-inch pieces and cook lightly in the butter, taking care to retain the onion's crisp texture. Leave to cool.

3　Rinse the potato and cut in half crosswise. Place in a microwave-safe bowl and cover. Microwave on medium for 2–3 minutes until cooked (some potatoes may take longer). Mash and leave to cool (do not add any butter or milk).

4　In a large bowl mix the chopped salmon and ground pork. Add the cooked onion, mashed potato and beaten egg, then season with salt and pepper. Combine all dressing ingredients.

5　Shape the mixture into 12 small burgers. Heat the oil in a frying pan. Place the burgers in the pan and cook evenly on both sides.

6　Serve on plates with dressing or other topping.

White Fish and Mozzarella Carpaccio Salad

This salad is a lovely combination of subtle flavors and colors. Raw fish work surprisingly well in this way. In the original recipe I used raw sea bream which I had previously wrapped in seaweed to give it more flavor. If you have the time to try this I have included the recipe below. Wrapping in kombu is a common method of preserving fish and it allows the fish to be eaten raw for up to two days, as well as adding extra taste and interest. You can use any sashimi-quality white fish for this recipe.

(Serves 4)
1 medium red onion
12 oz. seaweed-marinated sea bream sashimi
   (see below) or any other white fish sashimi
2 oz. mozzarella cheese
salt and coarsely ground black pepper
olive oil
lemon juice

1 Cut the red onion into wafer-thin half moon slices, and immerse in cold water for 5–10 minutes to remove any excess bitterness. Drain, pat dry and place on a serving plate.
2 Slice sea bream at an angle as thinly as you can manage (use your sharpest knife for this) and arrange the slices on top of the onion.
3 Place the mozzarella cheese on top, in the middle. Season with salt and pepper and drizzle over a little olive oil and fresh lemon juice.

(Serves 4)
12 oz. sashimi-quality piece of sea bream
   (you can also use other white fish sashimi)
1 teaspoon salt
2 pieces kombu seaweed of a suitable size
   to cover the fish

Seaweed-Marinated Sea Bream
1 Season both sides of the sea bream with the teaspoon of salt and leave for 1 hour.
2 Wash away the salt and wipe off the excess water.
3 Wash the kombu seaweed lightly and wipe off the excess water. Put the sea bream between two pieces of kombu seaweed and wrap in plastic wrap. Refrigerate for half a day. The flavor of the seaweed works really well with the sea bream.

Sautéed Squid Japanese Style
Ika no Sauté

Squid and octopus are both very popular in Japan and this is a very simple but tasty way to prepare squid.

(Serves 4)
¼ cup soy sauce
¼ cup mirin
1 teaspoon superfine sugar
1½ lbs. fresh squid
vegetable oil
chili powder or shichimi togarashi to taste
  (see Ingredients Note)

Ingredients Note:
Shichimi togarashi is a frequently used spice mix containing seven different spices like sansho (a Japanese pepper) and black sesame. However, the over-riding flavor is of chili.

1 Put the soy sauce, mirin and sugar into a small pan and bring to the boil over moderate heat. Then turn the heat down and simmer for 2–3 minutes. When you can see the sauce thickening a little bit, remove from the heat and let it cool.
2 Remove the squid tentacles and discard the intestinal sac. Wash the bodies and tentacles.
3 Marinate in the cooled sauce for about 30 minutes.
4 Sauté squid in a little oil in a frying pan over medium heat. Make sure that you don't overcook the squid and its tentacles, just cook until it changes color.
5 Once it's cooked, cut into thin rings and serve immediately with the chili powder or the shichimi togarashi.

Mackerel Grilled with Salt
Saba no Shio Yaki

There are several common ways of cooking fish in Japan; one way is with a teriyaki sauce, and another is with salt or "shio yaki." Despite being told to cut down on our salt intake, we really like this style of cooking and I think it is a good way to cook almost any type of fish. I often serve this with a wedge of "sudachi," which is one of the citrus fruits available in Japan and hard to find elsewhere. If you want to add a citrus flavor but can't find sudachi, use lime or lemon. Please note that although this recipe involves cooking the fish in an oven, it is also perfectly acceptable to grill the seasoned fish instead.

(Serves 4)
1¼ lbs. fresh mackerel fillets
salt and pepper
9 oz. bean sprouts
3 oz. snow peas
2 tablespoons sunflower or vegetable oil
1 clove garlic, thinly sliced
2 teaspoons soy sauce

1 Season the mackerel fillets with salt and pepper and place skin side up on a baking pan lined with waxed paper.
2 Bake in a preheated oven (450°F) for 15 to 20 minutes.
3 Prepare the bean sprouts by cutting off the tips (it makes a difference to the final taste). String the snow peas and blanch in a small pan of boiling water. Drain and then plunge in cold water for 5 minutes. Drain again, dry and then slice finely on the diagonal.
4 When the fish is almost ready to serve, cook the garlic in the oil in a frying pan or wok. When its aroma is released, add the bean sprouts and snow peas and cook quickly. Season with a little soy sauce and pepper.
5 Transfer the hot vegetables to a serving plate and place the mackerel fillets on top.

Tuna Carpaccio

It is amazing how many recipes can be created using raw fish. It's too easy to think only of eating it in the classical way with just wasabi and soy sauce. I hope that this recipe will help you see alternative ways of eating raw fish.

(Serves 4)
10 shiso leaves or a mix of fresh basil
    and mint leaves
6 oz. Japanese white daikon
    (mooli or Japanese white radish)
about 4 oz. sashimi-quality raw tuna
3 tablespoons mayonnaise
1 tablespoon milk
1 teaspoon light soy sauce
½ teaspoon mustard
a little white pepper

Ingredients Note:
Daikon is a large, white radish which is often served raw, either shredded or grated. It is sometimes known as mooli and can often be found in Chinese supermarkets or in other ethnic supermarkets. If you cannot find it a little shredded raw cabbage or even shredded iceberg or romaine lettuce would work.

1 Shred the shiso and daikon (mooli or Japanese white radish) and freshen by soaking in water for a minute, then gently squeeze to remove any excess water and put in a serving bowl.

2 Slice the tuna finely at an angle and arrange the slices on top of the salad.

3 Mix the mayonnaise, milk, light soy sauce, mustard and white pepper to make a dressing and drizzle it on top of the salad.

Octopus, Tomato and Parsley Salad

The sweetness of the tomatoes and the bitterness of the parsley bring out the flavor of the octopus in this recipe. Octopus can be a little tough so it is as well to make sure that it is cut into fairly small pieces. You could also use squid as a substitute in the same way. This goes very well with white wine.

(Serves 4)
8 oz. cooked octopus legs
4-6 small tomatoes
¾ cup parsley
3 tablespoons olive oil
2 tablespoons white wine vinegar
1 tablespoon balsamic vinegar
1 teaspoon light soy sauce
salt and pepper

Ingredients Note:
I like to mix these two different vinegars –
wine vinegar is a little too sharp on its own
and balsamic is too sweet – so mixing them
gives a well-balanced flavor to the dressing.
(See page 64 for how to cook octopus.)

1 Cut the octopus into 1-inch square pieces. Cut the tomatoes into pieces the same size as the octopus.
2 Discard the parsley stems and then roughly chop the leaves.
3 Mix the olive oil, white wine vinegar, balsamic vinegar, soy sauce and salt and pepper in a bowl. Add the octopus and the tomatoes.
4 Mix thoroughly and spoon onto a serving plate or bowl. Sprinkle the chopped parsley on top.

Salmon Teriyaki

This sauce has already proved to be popular around the world and you can buy the ready-made versions from most large supermarkets. However, it is such a simple sauce to make that it is worth making it yourself.

(Serves 4)
12 oz. fresh salmon
6-8 baby leeks
8 oz. eringi mushrooms
8 oz. maitake mushrooms
4½ tablespoons sunflower or vegetable oil
sudachi or lemon or lime
mustard

For the Teriyaki Sauce:
¼ cup soy sauce
1 tablespoon mirin
1 teaspoon superfine sugar

Ingredients Note:
You may not be able to find the eringi or maitake mushrooms so substitute other types of mushrooms that are available – most should work well with this salmon.

1 Marinate the salmon in the teriyaki sauce for an hour.
2 Cut the baby leeks into 1½-inch pieces. Slice the eringi mushrooms into 2–3 lengthwise pieces. Cut off the stalk of the maitake mushrooms.
3 Line a baking pan with waxed paper and place the salmon on it. Bake in a preheated oven (450°F) for 15 minutes, brushing the salmon with the sauce two or three times during cooking.
4 Put ½ tablespoon of the oil in a frying pan and add the baby leeks. Cook them over high heat and keep pressing them well into the pan to ensure that they cook. As they cook, they will become softer in texture – take them out when they are cooked to your taste.
5 Add the remaining oil and fry the mushrooms. When they are ready, place them and the leeks and the salmon on a plate and serve up with some sudachi and mustard.

Mackerel Tatsuta Age–Style
Saba no Tatsuta Age

Tatsuta age–style of cooking is suitable for chicken as well as for fish. It is very simple and tastes good even when cold, and makes a useful addition to lunchboxes.
Fish or meat is first marinated in sake, mirin and soy sauce and then dipped into potato starch and quickly fried. It should be nice and crispy on the outside but still very moist on the inside.

(Serves 4)
1 lb. fresh mackerel fillets
2 tablespoons sake
2 tablespoons soy sauce
½ tablespoon grated fresh ginger
1 tablespoon mirin
potato starch or cornstarch for coating
    the mackerel
oil for deep-frying
sudachi or lemon or lime
kinome (a Japanese herb) – if available or thinly
    sliced green onion

1 Check the fillets for bones and then cut them into bite-size pieces. Marinate them in the mix of sake, soy sauce, mirin and grated ginger for 10 minutes.
2 When you are ready to deep-fry the fish (which should be at room temperature), take them out of the marinade and dip them into plenty of potato starch. Fry the fish immediately to ensure that it goes crispy on the outside. The oil should be around 340°F and the fish should turn golden when cooked.
3 Serve immediately with wedges of sudachi, lemon or lime and the kinome leaves on top, if available.

Shrimp and Squid Tempura
Gochiso Kakiage

This mixture of shrimp, squid and leeks is best eaten piping hot. The main thing you should be aiming for is to make it really crispy. To do this you need to make the ingredients really cold before you deep-fry them – including, surprisingly enough, chilling the flour mix. As you will see from the photo we use this recipe to make four crunchy tempura disks or rounds that are served on top of a bowl of steaming hot rice. You can then either pour some of the tentsuyu sauce on top or have the sauce in a separate small bowl for each person to dip into. Alternatively, as with all types of tempura, you can dip into small dishes of salt and pepper or even chili powder instead.

(Serves 4)
6 oz. small shrimp
4 oz. fresh squid (without its tentacles)
6-8 baby leeks or green onions
2 oz. mitsuba (a Japanese herb like cilantro)
½ tablespoon baking powder
1 cup all-purpose flour
½ beaten egg
a little cold water
oil for deep-frying
2 tablespoons grated daikon
    (mooli or Japanese white radish)
2 teaspoons grated fresh ginger

For the Tentsuyu Tempura Dipping Sauce:
½ cup soy sauce
2 tablespoons sugar
¼ cup mirin
1 cup water
2 tablespoons dried fish flakes
dashi stock to dilute

1   Remove shrimp shells, tails and veins, and chop into 3–4
pieces. Take off the thin membrane from the squid, score the
surface with a knife then cut it into pieces of around 1¼ inch.
2   Chop the leeks or onions into 1¼-inch rounds and tear the
mitsuba leaves into pieces of about 1 inch.
3   Put the baking powder and flour into a plastic bag and shake.
Put the shrimp, squid, baby leeks and mitsuba into the
refrigerator for about half an hour to make sure they are
really cold.
4   Once suitably chilled, mix the shrimp, squid, leeks and
mitsuba with 2 tablespoons of the flour mix and form into a ball.
Put the remaining flour mix in a bowl, add ¾ cup of liquid
made up of half a beaten egg and cold water. Mix lightly.
5   Divide the shrimp, squid and leeks mixture into four, and shape
them roughly into flat rounds.
6   Heat the oil to 340°F. You can use a wok or a small saucepan
but you need to have enough oil to deep-fry one of the rounds
at a time.
7   Take a small plate and grease it with a little sunflower oil,
then place one of the rounds on top and pour over a quarter
of the batter. Mix the batter in lightly and then slide the round
into the oil.
8   Cook until the color changes, turning it halfway through
the cooking.
9   Repeat with the remaining three rounds.
10   Serve on hot rice with the tentsuyu sauce, some grated
daikon and grated ginger.

I hope you will use the best chicken and eggs you can find for the recipes in this section as there is such an enormous difference between just average and really good quality. Also, I think that the skin and thighs are the tastiest parts of the chicken, so in my recipes I encourage you to use them.

Most traditional restaurants in Japan specialize in a specific type of cooking. One of the most popular types is yakitori – chicken kebabs. These restaurants, often tiny places, serve up almost every part of a chicken on a skewer. You can order skewers of just chicken skin, chicken thighs or chicken livers – a huge variety is possible. These skewers are usually cooked over charcoal and served up with ice-cold mugs of beer – delicious.

In Japan we are quite happy to eat eggs raw. For breakfast it's quite common to crack an egg onto steaming hot rice and then we eat it with just a drizzle of soy sauce – the heat of the rice cooks the egg. When you eat sukiyaki (beef hot pot) you dip the hot beef slices into raw egg before eating it. However, if you are going to eat eggs raw just remember to make sure that they are absolutely fresh and of the highest quality (see Egg Safety, page 66).

Leaf-Wrapped Fried Chicken

Deep-fried chicken pieces are very popular in Japan. They are used in lunchboxes, in bars as accompaniments to drinks as well as for general family meals. This dish takes deep-fried chicken (tori no karaage) and serves it with fresh herbs and lettuce leaves. This allows everyone to make their own style of fried chicken roll – ready to dip into chili sauce.

(Serves 2–3)
10 oz. boneless chicken thighs with skin
3 tablespoons potato starch or cornflour
2 tablespoons all-purpose flour
sunflower or vegetable oil for deep-frying

For the marinade:
1 tablespoon soy sauce
½ tablespoon shokoshu (Chinese sake)
½ teaspoon crushed garlic
salt

fresh chives, mint, cilantro to taste
sweet chili sauce (for dipping)
some lettuce leaves to wrap the chicken

1 First make up the marinade. Pierce the chicken skin in several places before cutting each piece into 6 to 7 smaller pieces. Place them in the marinade and make sure that they are all well coated and leave them to marinate for around 30 minutes.

2 Lightly mix the potato starch and flour and then dust the marinated chicken pieces generously.

3 Heat the oil for frying (340°F). When the oil is hot enough, deep-fry the chicken pieces for 4–5 minutes until crisp, golden and cooked through. To maintain the oil temperature, do not add too many chicken pieces at once (halve one chicken piece to check if it is cooked inside). Drain the cooked chicken on paper towels.

4 Serve the deep-fried chicken with a selection of washed herbs and lettuce leaves. Wrap pieces of chicken in the leaves accompanied by herbs of your choice. Using your fingers to eat, dip in chili sauce and enjoy!

Chicken Sauté Kari Kari Style

Crispy chicken is great with a mountain of chives on top. Use so many chives that you can hardly see the chicken underneath. This recipe also works well with duck or with chicken breast, if you prefer.

(Serves 4)
10 oz. boneless chicken thighs with skin
salt and pepper
½ tablespoon sunflower or vegetable oil
3 oz. chives
ponzu soy sauce (see page 80)
mustard

1 Prick the skin of the chicken with a fork then dry with paper towels. Season with salt and pepper.
2 Heat the oil in a frying pan and fry the chicken skin side down. When it turns golden brown turn it over and continue to cook, covering the chicken with a drop lid or circle of foil to keep it moist – see the Beef on Rice recipe (p. 59) for more information.
3 Chop the chives finely.
4 Cut the cooked chicken into bite-size pieces, sprinkle with plenty of chives, pour over a little ponzu soy sauce and serve with a little mustard on the side.

Rice Topped with Raw Egg
Tamago Gake Gohan

This is such an easy meal – the original Japanese fast food! Although it's simple it's very tasty and one of my favorite ways to eat egg. It is also a very traditional dish for breakfast. This recipe uses quite a few typically Japanese toppings, so if you can't find them then try substituting them with what you can find locally.

(Serves 4)
3 cups hot cooked rice
4 fresh eggs (see Egg Safety, page 66.)
a little soy sauce

Suggested Traditional Toppings:
seaweed paste (iwa nori)
dried fish flakes
dried baby anchovies (chirimen zansho)
Japanese pickles
asari clams boiled down in soy (see the
   Maze Gohan recipe on page 60)

Ingredients Note:
Instead of the traditional toppings you can use ingredients you already have on hand like cooked spinach, salmon or canned tuna. You can even have it with just the egg and soy sauce.

1 Fill a rice bowl with freshly cooked rice, crack an egg on top, then add your preferred toppings. Add the soy sauce and mix well.

Steamed Chicken Salad with Sesame Sauce

Mushi Dori no Gomadare Salad

Sesame sauce using the juices from cooked chicken is so easy to prepare. This style of dressing with sesame, gomadare, is very common in Japanese cooking and is used for both meat and vegetables. This particular chicken dish makes a lovely appetizer, but it also goes very well with cold noodles.

(Serves 4)

3-4 green onions
salt and pepper
2 small cucumbers
10 oz. boneless chicken thighs with skin
1 tablespoon sake
1 teaspoon sesame oil
small piece of crushed ginger

For the Sesame Sauce:
¼ cup liquid made up from the juices
  of the cooked chicken (and water if necessary)
4 tablespoons sesame paste
2 tablespoons soy sauce
2 tablespoons superfine sugar
½ tablespoon rice vinegar
2 teaspoons chili paste or to-ban-jan
2 tablespoons roughly ground sesame seeds
2 tablespoons finely shredded green onions
2 teaspoons finely chopped ginger
2 teaspoons finely chopped garlic

Ingredients Note:
Gomadare —meaning "dressed with sesame sauce"—can be made either with ready-made sesame paste or, more traditionally, by grinding toasted sesame seeds to a rough paste in a suribachi (pestle and mortar). Tahini, a Greek-style sesame paste is a reasonable and easily available substitute, but as it is not made from toasted sesame there is a slight difference in flavor. Unsweetened peanut butter is another possible substitute.

1 Finely chop the green onion diagonally, reserving the green part for use during cooking the chicken. Soak in cold water for a few minutes to remove the bitterness of the onion, then drain and put aside to use later.

2 On a chopping board, sprinkle the cucumbers with a few pinches of salt, rubbing it into the flesh, then rinse. This lessens the aroma of the cucumber and gives it a good green color. Hit the cucumbers with a pestle (if you don't have a pestle, use a bottle) and break it apart with your hands, to make uneven pieces.

3 Pierce the chicken pieces with a skewer and place in a microwave-safe bowl. Add the salt, pepper and oil and then place the green part of the green onion and the crushed ginger on top. Cover and microwave on medium for 4 minutes or until cooked. Leave to cool. Keep the juice from the chicken to use in the sesame sauce.

4 Shred the chicken with your hands and place in a serving dish. Mix in the cucumber and put the chopped green onion on top.

5 Mix all the ingredients for the sesame sauce in a small bowl and pour over the chicken and cucumber.

Chicken and French Beans with Basil Rice
Tori Adobo fu

I use a lot of green beans in my recipes as I love their taste, color and crunch. In this recipe I use the slightly larger French beans but any green bean will be good. This meal goes well with boiled rice, but if served with basil rice it becomes even more of a feast.

(Serves 4)
1 lb. boneless chicken thighs with skin
pepper
4 cloves garlic
12 oz. French beans
½ tablespoon sunflower oil or vegetable oil
½ cup rice vinegar
¼ cup sake
1½ cups water
½ cup soy sauce
1 bay leaf
1 teaspoon ground coriander
4 hard-cooked eggs (shelled)

1 Cut the chicken into 6 pieces. Season lightly with pepper. Peel the garlic cloves.
2 Remove the strings from the French beans, trim the ends and then lightly boil or steam. Drain while the beans are still very firm. Cut each bean into 3.
3 Heat the oil in a frying pan or wok over moderate heat. Add the garlic, and when its aroma is released place the chicken, skin side down, into the pan. When the skin turns golden brown turn and brown the other side.
4 Add the rice vinegar, sake, water, soy sauce, bay leaf and coriander to the pan and simmer at low to moderate heat.
5 When the liquid has reduced by half, add the boiled eggs and the French beans. Simmer for 5 minutes and then serve.

Basil Rice:
(Serves 4)
2 handfuls fresh basil
2 tablespoons sunflower or vegetable oil
2 tablespoons finely chopped garlic
2 cups hot cooked rice – preferably Japanese rice
1 teaspoon granulated chicken stock
salt and pepper

1 Roughly chop the basil.
2 Heat the oil in a frying pan over moderate heat. Add the garlic and fry gently. When you can smell the garlic, add the cooked rice and fry until heated through. Season with the granulated stock, salt and pepper. Turn off the heat and mix in the basil. Serve immediately.

Chicken with Red and Green Peppers

Tori to Piman no Itame ni

This is a really quick and delicious meal. The red and green peppers add a lovely color but make sure not to overcook them – they should still have quite a bite to them. I like to serve this up with some Japanese white rice.

(Serves 4)
1 lb. boneless chicken thighs with skin
½ cup finely chopped onion
1 tablespoon finely chopped garlic
¼ cup red wine
¼ cup soy sauce
fresh basil and rosemary
1 medium green pepper
½ large red pepper
2 tablespoons olive or sunflower oil

1 Cut the chicken into 1-inch pieces. In a bowl, mix together the onion, garlic, red wine, soy sauce, basil and rosemary and use this as a marinade for the chicken while you prepare the peppers.
2 Cut the peppers in half and remove the seeds, then cut them lengthwise into fairly thin strips.
3 Heat half of the olive oil (1 tablespoon) in a frying pan over medium heat. Put in the chicken and brown on both sides, then cook over medium heat until just cooked through. Remove from the pan.
4 Add the remaining oil and quickly fry the peppers. When they are just cooked, though still with a bite to them, return the chicken and any marinade sauce that remains, and heat through. Serve hot.

Japanese-Style Savory Pancake
Okonomiyaki Hiroshima fu

Anyone who has been to Japan will probably have tasted okonomiyaki. It is a cheap, popular family style of eating. There are many different recipes for okonomiyaki, with ingredients varying from region to region and household to household. Everyone has their favorite and mine is one that comes from the Hiroshima area. I love it so much that I will even travel to Hiroshima just to be able to eat their special okonomiyaki!

Okonomiyaki is not a simple dish to make for the first time but it is worth trying and is almost a complete meal in itself. If you can get a tabletop burner it is fun to cook this at the table with friends or family.

If this is the first time you have made these, it might be useful for you to imagine the final dish. Working from the bottom up, there is a pancake filled with cabbage, squid and pork, a layer of fried noodles and finally a couple of fried eggs on top. Quite a feast.

1 To make the batter: sift the flour and baking soda into a bowl. Add the water and mirin and mix well.

2 Heat a little oil in an 8-inch frying pan over moderate heat. Pour in enough batter to make a thin pancake.

3 Sprinkle a quarter of the chopped cabbage, bean sprouts, green onions, dried fish flakes and chopped pork onto the batter. Season lightly with salt and pepper. Put the squid on top and cook – making sure that the pork and squid are properly cooked before going to the next stage.

4 Add 2 tablespoons of batter to the pancake then turn over and press lightly using a spatula.

5 In a separate frying pan heat a little more oil, then add the cooked noodles and fry lightly. Season with 1 tablespoon Worcestershire sauce, shape the noodles into a circle and transfer the previously cooked pancake on top.

6 Fry two eggs then put the pancake and noodles on top of the eggs and turn the whole thing over. Turn out onto a plate so that the eggs are on the top and the noodles underneath. Repeat this procedure using the rest of the ingredients.

7 To serve: mix the tonkatsu sauce, Worcestershire sauce and tomato ketchup and drizzle over the assembled pancake. If you have ao-nori seaweed, sprinkle it over and add the red ginger for garnish.

(Serves 4)
For the pancake batter:
1 cup all-purpose flour
⅓ teaspoon baking soda
1 cup water
1 teaspoon mirin

For the pancake filling:
a little sunflower or vegetable oil
2 cups shredded sweetheart or green cabbage
9 oz. bean sprouts
finely chopped green onions or chives to taste
dried fish flakes to taste
4 oz. thinly sliced uncooked pork
salt and pepper
6 oz. thinly sliced squid (or to taste)
about 20 oz. cooked Chinese egg noodles
4 tablespoons Worcestershire sauce
8 eggs
4 tablespoons tonkatsu sauce to taste
2 teaspoons Worcestershire sauce
1 tablespoon ketchup
red pickled ginger (beni shoga) and ao-nori
   to taste

Ingredients Note:
Ao-nori seaweed is a green dried seaweed often sprinkled on food to give extra flavor. Tonkatsu sauce is a rich, dark sauce that can be obtained in Asian supermarkets.

Beef & Pork

Despite the fact that I love vegetables, I also really love meat. Steak is one of my three favorite dishes (the others being sashimi and tori no karaage). I just love steak – sirloin and fillet, thick cut, rare or thinly sliced – I could eat it any way. My husband is more particular and loves his beef thinly sliced and cooked in a traditional Japanese style such as shabu shabu (beef and vegetables cooked in boiling water) or as sukiyaki (a type of beef stew).

Even though we've only been eating beef in Japan for just over 150 years it's now become very popular, and good-quality beef is inexpensive and easy to obtain. I often get some reasonably priced beef from the local supermarket and turn it into something interesting using a variety of seasonings – sometimes I cook it Japanese style, sometimes western style and sometimes Asian style. Beef can also be transformed by the types of vegetables you cook it with, and I love creating new recipes to change ordinary beef into something really special.

Pork is widely used in Japan and is often deep-fried and served with tonkatsu, or fried on a skewer with onions and vegetables, as kushikatsu and sometimes sautéed.

Ground meat is also very popular and used in many ways. It is usually sold as a mix of beef and pork. Since the war, hamburgers have become an increasingly normal part of our culture, but usually served with a Japanese twist – covered with a sauce or a fried egg – a little different from hamburgers American style.

Rare Beef Salad
Gyu Tataki Salad

Tataki style is a very common way of serving beef and some "meatier" fish like tuna. It involves searing the meat or fish very quickly, then slicing it and eating it with tangy dipping sauces. This recipe is great for dinner parties as it can easily be prepared in advance. The dipping sauce, the mentsuyu, can also be made in advance and kept until needed.

(Serves 4)
1 lb. beef roast (preferably round)
salt and pepper to season
1 teaspoon crushed garlic
sunflower or vegetable oil
2-3 inch daikon (mooli or Japanese white radish)
small bunch of mitsuba (or cilantro if unavailable)
5 shiso leaves or a mix of fresh mint and basil
1 bud of myoga – or 1–2 green onions
mustard to taste

For the Mentsuyu Sauce:
1 cup soy sauce
½ cup mirin
3 tablespoons superfine sugar
1 cup water
2½ tablespoons dried fish flakes

Ingredients Note:
If you are unable to find these particular leaves for the salad, then use anything available, choosing textures that are crunchy and flavors that are sharp and tangy, such as arugula.

If you cannot find the dried fish flakes, substitute the ½ cup of water for ½ cup of fish stock. It should not be a strong fishy flavor but just have a slight tang.

1 Make sure that the beef is at room temperature before you start. Season the roast with salt, pepper and garlic.

2 In a wok, heat the oil until very hot, then put the beef in and seal it on all sides. Remember that the beef will keep on cooking even after you have taken it out of the pan so adjust the cooking time accordingly.

3 Take the roast out of the pan and wrap it in foil.

4 Chop up the daikon into thin matchsticks. Cut the mitsuba into 1-inch-length pieces. Take the shiso leaves and first cut them in two down the center and then chop them up finely.

5 If you have myoga slice it finely, or use finely chopped green onions. Put the myoga in water for a couple of minutes then drain and dry well.

6 Now take all the chopped leaves and mix them. Take the beef, slice it finely and place the slices on top of the greens. Finish by dabbing some mustard on the beef slices.

7 To make the mentsuyu sauce: take all the ingredients and put them in a microwave-safe bowl without a lid and cook on medium for 3 minutes. Leave to cool and strain. Refrigerate until required.

Steak Marinated in Two Types of Miso

Miso is not just for soups, it makes a tasty marinade for both fish and meat.
For this recipe I use two types of miso, the sweeter white miso and the saltier red miso. I usually make my own miso each January or February, making enough for the whole year. Although miso is excellent for health, it can be a little salty, so you need to be careful not to overdo it.

(Serves 2)
3½ tablespoons white miso
3½ tablespoons red miso
½ tablespoon soy sauce
½ tablespoon sake
1 tablespoon mirin
8 oz. beef fillet
sunflower or vegetable oil to pan-fry the meat
wasabi to taste

1 Mix together the two types of miso, soy sauce, sake and mirin. Using a tablespoon of this sauce, marinate the fillet and wrap in plastic wrap and refrigerate for 2–3 hours. (You can keep the remaining marinade sauce for up to four weeks in the refrigerator; it doesn't change in flavor.)
2 About half an hour before you want to cook it take the meat out of the refrigerator, so that it reaches room temperature.
3 Heat a little oil in a frying pan. Remove any excess marinade from the fillet and then pan-fry over high heat.
4 When cooked (according to your own taste) serve garnished with some wasabi. I often serve this with a green salad and some rice that I have shaped in a ramekin and decorated with toasted sesame seeds.

Beef and Vegetable Rolls
Gyuniku no Yasai Maki

I think it is a very Asian tendency to wrap things – the spring roll is a great example of this. This recipe uses beef instead of pastry as a wrap, and it works just as well with thinly sliced pork. The sauce is also so good that you can just marinate the beef in it and then cook and eat it as it is.

(Serves 4)
Sauce for the beef:
4 tablespoons soy sauce
1 tablespoon sake
2 tablespoons sesame oil
2 tablespoons superfine sugar
2 tablespoons red wine
3 tablespoons ground sesame seeds
2 teaspoons finely crushed garlic
1 teaspoon grated fresh ginger
black pepper
chili pepper or ichimi togarashi

8 oz. fresh green asparagus
3 oz. green beans
12 oz. thinly sliced beef

1 Put all the ingredients for the sauce into a bowl and mix well, making sure the sugar dissolves. Leave it to mature for 2–3 hours.
2 Cut off the woody base and strip the side leaves from the asparagus. Remove ends from the green beans. Steam the vegetables so they are still firm to the bite. Drain. Plunge into chilled water and drain again.
3 Pour around ¼ cup of the sauce onto the beef and mix it in thoroughly by hand.
4 Spread the beef slices out on a plate. Place a spear of asparagus and some green beans down the center of each slice and then roll the beef around the vegetables, making a sausage shape. If there are not enough vegetables, then just roll some of the beef slices.
5 As the beef is so thin, these rolls cook very quickly. You can either grill them or pan-fry them. You might find it easier if you put a skewer through them but they should stay together anyway.
6 Carefully cut the rolls into bite-size pieces and place on a serving plate. Pour over the remaining sauce and serve with white rice.

Pot Roast Pork

I find this method of cooking a large pork roast is the best – it remains more tender than if roasted in the oven. It is not something that I would do every day but it is great when you want to entertain, and any leftovers can be used in fried rice (chahan) or even in sandwiches.

(Serves 8)
4 lbs. boneless pork roast – preferably shoulder
salt and coarsely ground black pepper to taste
string to tie the roast
½ tablespoon sunflower or vegetable oil
3–4 bay leaves

Japanese-Style Wasabi Sauce:
1 cup of juices made up from the cooked
    pork roast and chicken stock
1 tablespoon of cornstarch or potato starch mixed
    with 1 tablespoon of cold water
2 tablespoons soy sauce
1 teaspoon wasabi

1 Season the roast with salt and pepper. Tie with string.
2 Put the oil in a large frying pan over very high heat.
3 Place the roast in the pan and sear on all sides.
4 Remove from the heat and place in a very heavy Dutch oven with a lid (I find that a Le Creuset is perfect for this). Put the bay leaves on top and cover loosely with some aluminium foil – this helps to keep the moisture in.
5 Cover with the lid and cook over very low heat for about an hour, turning the meat once or twice during this period.
6 After checking that the meat is cooked (the juices should run clear when you put in a skewer) take the roast out of the pan and let it cool. When cooled, slice it as thinly as you can.
7 To make the Japanese-style wasabi sauce, take the juices from the cooked roast, skim off the fat and then add some chicken stock to make up a cup of stock. Add the cornstarch, and heat in a pan. When it starts to thicken, add the soy sauce. Finally add the wasabi. Place in a small pitcher and serve with the sliced roast pork.

Alternative dressing: Apple Mayonnaise Sauce:
   Take 3 medium-size apples and peel, core and then cut them into 8 wedges. Put 1 cup of wine and ¼ cup of water into a pan and bring to a boil. Add the apple, cover with a drop lid or circle of foil, and simmer gently until most of the liquid has been absorbed and the apples are soft. Turn over once during cooking. Leave to cool.
   Then blend together the apple, 3–4 tablespoons mayonnaise, 1 tablespoon finely chopped onion and salt and pepper to taste. If you are feeling lazy you can make this with purchased applesauce, but this method gives better results.

Japanese Pepper Steak with Ginger Mashed Potatoes

Japanese sansho pepper is different from black pepper in both aroma and flavor. Unfortunately, it is not very easy to find outside of Japan and China. The nearest seasoning that I can find is Szechuan pepper, so use that if you can't find sansho.

1   Make sure that the steaks are at room temperature and then season on both sides with a little salt and then lots of the sansho or Szechuan pepper.

2   Heat the oil in a frying pan and cook the steak to your liking.

3   Place the steak on a plate with a sprig of kinome on top. If you cannot find kinome then use a little cress. Serve with the ginger mashed potatoes.

Ginger Mashed Potatoes

1   Peel the potatoes and cut each one into 4. Soak in water for a few minutes then drain and dry.

2   Line a microwave-safe bowl with paper towels and add the potatoes. Lightly cover and microwave on medium for 5 minutes, or until cooked through.

3   Take the potatoes out while they are still hot and mash. Add the butter and milk and mix thoroughly. Add the cream and season with salt and pepper.

4   Put the soy sauce and mirin into a small pan and bring to the boil. Add the potato starch and simmer until thickened. Remove from the heat and mix in the grated ginger.

5   Place the mashed potato on a plate, make a hollow in the center and pour in the ginger sauce to serve.

(Serves 4)
4 (6-oz.) beef fillets (1 inch thick)
a little salt
plenty of coarsely ground sansho pepper
  or Szechuan pepper to taste
sunflower or vegetable oil for pan frying
kinome leaf if available

Ginger Mashed Potatoes:
(Serves 4)
4 medium-size potatoes
2 tablespoons butter
½ cup milk
¼ cup heavy cream
salt and pepper
¼ cup soy sauce
¼ cup mirin
1 small tablespoon potato starch or cornstarch
  mixed with 1 tablespoon water
1 tablespoon grated fresh ginger

Bite-Size Steak Pieces with Japanese Vegetables
Koro Koro Steak Tataki fu

This steak dish makes a light and tasty meal and is good not only to eat but also to look at. This original recipe uses many Japanese vegetable ingredients but if you cannot find some of them then use what you have locally such as watercress, cilantro, parsley or radish. This meal is also very good for those using chopsticks – you don't need a knife to eat it.

(Serves 4)
about 2 lbs. sirloin steaks (1-inch thick if possible)
a little sunflower or vegetable oil for pan frying
2 tablespoons finely chopped ginger
¼ cup chopped myoga if available
¼ cup green onions or chives – chopped
¼ cup chopped celery
small bunch of shredded shiso leaves or a mix
   of fresh basil and mint leaves
dashi shoyu sauce to taste (see Ingredients Note)
grated daikon (mooli or Japanese white radish)
   to taste

Ingredients Note:
To make dashi shoyu: Combine ¼ cup dashi (fish stock) with ¼ cup soy sauce (half and half) and add 1 tablespoon rice vinegar. Heat, then allow to cool before use.

1 Cut the steak into bite-size pieces.
2 Heat the oil in a frying pan and quickly cook the steak cubes, browning on all sides.
3 In a bowl combine the chopped vegetables (except the daikon).
4 When the steak is cooked to your liking, place on a serving dish and scatter the chopped vegetables on top.
5 Make the dashi shoyu sauce and pour it over the steak pieces. Eat accompanied by a small amount of the grated daikon.

Shabu Shabu–Style Beef

This style of cuisine is called nabe ryori (casserole cooking) and is a very relaxing way to eat, sitting around a bubbling casserole dish, cooking at the table. In Japan we have restaurants that specialize in this one dish, serving only shabu shabu all year round. The ingredients are not only meat or fish but always include a variety of vegetables. After you've assembled the ingredients the cooking itself is simple and easy.

This dish is always cooked on a tabletop gas or electric burner. The cooking starts with the meat, then adding the tofu and finally the vegetables. Once we have eaten the meat and vegetables we add rice or noodles to the liquid, which by now is full of goodness and flavor. This nabe (casserole)-style cuisine is great for dinner parties. As with many other recipes, we use a variety of sauces to dip the cooked meat, vegetables or tofu into, and here I have included two.

(Serves 4)
For the stock:
2 sheets kombu seaweed about 4-inch square
  to make the dashi stock
7 cups water

3 oz. dried kuzukiri (Japanese noodles –
  (see Ingredients Note)
1 (12.3 oz.) box soft silken tofu
8 oz. mizuna (a Japanese herb –
  see Ingredients Note)
8 oz. baby leeks
1 lb. finely sliced beef
sesame dipping sauce
ponzu soy dipping sauce
about 12 oz. ready-cooked udon noodles

1 Wipe the kombu seaweed lightly to remove excess salt and then soak it in the water for 30 minutes.

2 In a separate pan boil a large quantity of water for the noodles. Cook over a moderate heat, following the instructions on the package. Drain when cooked.

3 Drain and then wrap the tofu in paper towels to remove excess water, then cut into large bite-size pieces.

4 Chop the mizuna into 3-inch pieces and slice the baby leeks diagonally into 1-inch pieces.

5 Arrange the beef, mizuna, baby leeks, cooked noodles and tofu attractively onto a large plate, keeping the different ingredients separate, as they will be cooked at different stages.

6 Prepare the sesame dipping sauce, the ponzu soy dipping sauce and condiments as described below.

7 Pour the soup stock into a heavy saucepan until ⅔ full and heat. Once it comes to the boil, turn down the heat and dip in the beef, slice by slice.

8 The beef will cook quickly so have a plate ready to put the cooked beef onto. Let everyone help themselves and dip the beef into the dipping sauces.

Ingredients Note:
Increasingly you can find kombu seaweed (kelp) in large supermarkets but if you cannot find it then make the initial broth with fish stock seasoned with a little chicken stock.

The kuzukiri noodles are unique to Japan but I think you could substitute Thai glass noodles instead. The main thing is that you use noodles that do not have a strong flavor but have a lovely smooth texture. Mizuna is a green vegetable. I suggest that you use another green leafy vegetable like spinach or arugula, if you can't find mizuna locally.

Sesame Dipping Sauce

Sesame dipping sauce is essential for shabu shabu. This handmade sauce is very full-bodied and smells superb.

6 tablespoons sesame paste
2 tablespoons soy sauce
1 tablespoon rice vinegar
1 tablespoon superfine sugar
1 teaspoon granulated chicken stock dissolved
   in ¼ cup hot water
coarsely ground sesame seeds

To make sesame sauce: In a bowl combine the sesame paste, soy sauce, vinegar, sugar and a mixture of hot chicken stock (making sure it's dissolved). Mix well. Add some ground sesame, if you like. I think it adds to the flavor.

For the ponzu soy dipping sauce: Make the ponzu sauce according to the recipe for Tofu and Ponzu Soy Sauce (page 81). To this add, according to your own taste; the juice from 4–5 sudachi or limes, ½ cup chopped green onions or chives, some grated daikon (mooli), some coarsely ground sesame seeds and chili powder (shichimi togarashi).

9 Using a spoon, add the tofu to the saucepan and bring the soup back to a gentle boil, then add the remaining vegetables and the cooked noodles. Add more stock if needed and, as it cooks, eat as before.

10 When the meat and vegetables are finished you can add the precooked udon noodles (thick white Japanese noodles); they absorb the flavors of the enriched stock and are really delicious.

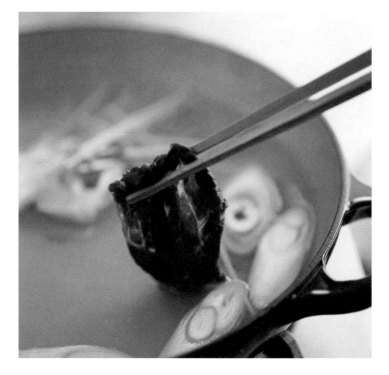

Sushi

All countries have their national dish – Japan's is sushi. It was originally created as a way of preserving fish but has subsequently become food that you eat on important occasions or when you have a special visitor. It is associated with fun and happy moments in life.

Its popularity is no longer limited to Japan. It seems to have captured the imagination of the world and now can be found outside Japan in many places, including the refrigerated, ready-to-eat food sections of supermarkets.

I think that people are interested in the variety that sushi offers. It can be made into individual small balls of sushi rice with various toppings (nigiri style); it can be made into one large serving of sushi rice with various toppings (chirashi style); or it can be made into long rolls stuffed with different ingredients and then cut up into bite-size pieces (maki style).

Nigiri zushi is considered to be best when it's created by professionals, who spend years training to cook the rice, slice the fish and put it all together. However, many Japanese households make chirashi zushi and maki zushi at home for parties and special occasions. I have created recipes for all types of sushi, nigiri, chirashi and maki, which can be easily replicated and don't require years of training.

How to Make Sushi Rice

I have used many illustrations to show you how varied sushi can be. You can make individual balls with different toppings (nigiri zushi), you can make large bowls of rice with different toppings (chirashi zushi) or you can make long sushi rolls with different fillings which are cut into smaller rounds (maki zushi). It is a remarkably flexible dish.

One of the most important elements in sushi is the sushi rice itself, which is the usual Japanese short-grain rice mixed with sweetened rice vinegar. You need to cook the rice with a little less water than usual as you will be adding the vinegar dressing while the rice is still warm and absorbent.

The best sushi rice is served when it is still ever so slightly warm, so avoid chilling it if possible. All references to rice in this chapter are to sushi rice; that is to say rice that has been dressed with sushi vinegar (you might like to note that sushi, as a word, becomes zushi after certain vowels).

Sushi Vinegar Dressing

Mix 1 cup rice vinegar with 3½ tablespoons superfine sugar in a small nonaluminium saucepan. Heat until the sugar has dissolved and then add 2 teaspoons salt and ⅓ teaspoon kombu cha powder, mix and allow to cool down. You can refrigerate this for 4–5 days before use. If you can't find the kombu cha powder then use a little more salt to taste.

1²/₃ cups uncooked rice and an equal amount of water by volume (makes 20–24 nigiri-style small balls, 1 bowl of chirashi zushi, 4 maki roles or 6 ura maki rolls)

Sushi Rice

Cook in the same way as regular rice (either in a rice cooker, microwave or saucepan). When cooked transfer into a large shallow bowl or a wooden sushi pot and, while cooling, drizzle on about ¾ cup of the sushi vinegar dressing (to taste) and fold in using a cutting and folding action – trying to make sure that you do not break the rice which would make it sticky. At the same time fan the rice to help speed the cooling process. When cool, use in your chosen sushi style.

Useful Ingredients

Even though sushi can be created in many different ways, there are certain ingredients which are always useful.

Wasabi   I come from an area of Japan where wasabi is grown. It is only possible to grow wasabi in really clean, pure water. The root is grated and made into a paste – rather like a mustard. Wasabi is extensively used in sushi making – its fiery taste helps to cut through the rice's slight sweetness. Wasabi is now becoming more easily available internationally, though usually in a tube or in powdered form. It is definitely worth tracking down.

Nori   We often use these crispy, shiny sheets of dried seaweed for sushi. It is a must for the maki style of sushi but it is also used chopped and sprinkled onto the chirashi style of sushi and with nigiri style. Sometimes we have "roll your own" parties where we just put out all the ingredients and people make their own "cones" of sushi (temaki zushi) using a sheet of nori as a wrap.

Shiso leaves   These aromatic leaves are commonly served with sushi and with sashimi.

Gari   This pickled ginger is always served with nigiri-style sushi mainly to cleanse the palate in between servings. It is very simple to make. Take a piece of really fresh ginger (around 2 inches), peel, then slice very thinly with the grain. Sprinkle with a little salt and leave for 5–10 minutes, then put into boiling water to soften, and finally wash. Next soak it for 4 hours in a mix of ½ cup sushi vinegar and 1 tablespoon superfine sugar. Drain off any excess liquid, pat dry and use as required.

Sesame seeds   These are useful both to sprinkle on, or mix with, rice but are often used to roll "inside-out" maki zushi rolls in. They are sold in Japan already lightly toasted.

Suggested Toppings or Fillings

When you choose a topping think about what will bring the flavor to life – sometimes it needs a dab of wasabi, sometimes some grated ginger. As you become more familiar with the flavors, you will find what works well for you.

Sashimi Raw fish. Most people associate sushi with raw fish – though it is not necessarily so. The easiest sashimi to work with is probably either tuna or salmon as neither of these fish are very strong tasting when raw. Almost any type of raw fish can be used, providing it is really fresh and that it is sliced in a way that makes it easy to eat. Ask your fishmonger for advice.

Cooked Fish Traditionally, we do not use much cooked fish in sushi but king prawns are often used cooked. You can also use smoked fish, like smoked salmon or smoked eel.

Fish Roe This can be used either as a main ingredient or as decoration.

Meat I have included two illustrations using chicken. You can also use rare beef or even duck but make sure it is thinly sliced so it is easy to eat.

Omelette A sweetened omelette provides not only taste but also an attractive color. To make it, take three eggs, beat gently with a fork, add 1 tablespoon sugar and a little salt. Cook as you would do with an ordinary omelette. You can then shred this for the chirashi zushi or cut it into strips for the nigiri or maki style of sushi. Adjust the thickness according to your own taste, although for the chirashi zushi the omlette must be very thin.

Vegetables Many vegetables can be used with sushi, either cooked or raw. Most commonly used are cucumbers, avocados and chives.

Nigiri Style Sushi

Nigiri zushi is the type of sushi where a slice of fish, meat, omelette or vegetable is placed on a small ball of rice. Most people think this is the only type of sushi possible but, as you will see, it is not.

I often make these sushi rice balls using plastic wrap to shape them – it is easier than doing it with your hands, especially if they are warm.

Tori, Kyuri no Nigiri Zushi

This has to be the easiest sushi in the world, using boiled breast of chicken, avocado and cucumber. Cut the chicken, avocado and cucumber into strips. Dab wasabi on each of the balls of rice, follow this with a strip of cucumber or avocado and then a piece of chicken. Put a little dressing on the chicken (2 tablespoons each of mirin and soy sauce combined with 2 teaspoons of superfine sugar cooked for 2½ minutes in a microwave and then cooled) and wrap in nori seaweed.

Temari Style Zushi

For this sushi I have used egg topped with cod roe, white fish sashimi topped with grated ginger and green onions, tuna sashimi and some cooked, sliced chicken (see recipe below).

9 oz. boneless chicken thigh with skin
1 tablespoon mirin
1 tablespoon soy sauce
2 teaspoons superfine sugar
Fry the chicken skin side down until brown and crispy,
    turn over and add the mirin, soy sauce and sugar.
    Fry until the chicken is cooked through.
Take out and allow to cool before slicing thinly.

Oba Zushi

Oba is another name for shiso, so this sushi is called "oba zushi." I like to mix in a tablespoon of lightly toasted white sesame seeds into the sushi rice before making the balls. I then top these with thinly sliced sea bream dabbed with wasabi, ham with a dab of mayonnaise, smoked eel topped with some ground sansho or Szechuan pepper or smoked salmon. On top of each piece of sushi I then place a shiso leaf. Ideally, I like to make these balls a little flat by placing them in a dish and pressing down with a plate to flatten them slightly. Serve with a little soy sauce and sudachi juice or lime juice. (I like to use the sea bream that has been marinated in kombu seaweed. See page 87, White Fish and Mozzarella Carpaccio Salad.)

Chirashi Zushi

This is great for parties. Although it is better to use sushi rice for the recipe, it is possible to use long-grain rice as it is served in a bowl or a large plate, and is not shaped in the way that nigiri zushi or maki zushi are. Here I used 6-8 ounces cooked shrimp, 8 ounces smoked salmon, 8 ounces sashimi-quality tuna and 4 ounces sashimi-quality white fish. Then I scattered some ribbons of sweetened omelette over and mixed in some shredded carrots cooked with sugar, soy sauce and zucchini. Garnish it with salmon roe. You can use almost anything that you believe will work well together on this dish – both raw and cooked.

Maki Zushi

A rolling mat is a great help for this kind of sushi but if you cannot find one then you can use a similar-sized square of waxed paper. Make sure you have all the ingredients ready to use before you start to construct the maki zushi. Use a sharp knife to cut it, and keep a bowl of water handy to wet the knife and your fingers, to stop the rice sticking.
I find that 8 ounces of sashimi-quality tuna is about right for 4 rolls, using 1½ cups uncooked rice to ⅓ cup sushi vinegar.

Maki Zushi

1 Take ½ sheet of nori seaweed and place it on the rolling mat. Spread a thin layer of cooked rice evenly over the nori, leaving ½-inch of nori on each side free from rice as you will need this to seal the roll. Dab a little wasabi in a line across the rice – be careful not to use too much as it is very spicy.

2 Place the ingredients on the wasabi, but not too many or it won't roll well. For this roll use sashimi-quality tuna, roughly shredded shiso leaves and finely julienned cucumber.

3 Roll it carefully and evenly away from you, pressing it firmly. Remove the rolling mat, trim any ingredients that are protruding from the ends of the roll and cut into about 1-inch pieces.

Ura Maki Zushi (inside-out roll)

1 Place ½ sheet of nori on the nonstick parchment paper and evenly spread a thin layer of fresh sushi rice across it (don't leave the edges free on this one). Carefully turn it over so the nori is facing upwards and add the ingredients. For this roll use crab sticks (about 8 oz.), avocado and shiso leaves.

2 Use mayonnaise instead of wasabi, and dab on top of the ingredients. Roll carefully and evenly away from you.

3 Put some toasted sesame seeds on a plate and roll the sushi in them, so the roll is well coated.

4 Using a sharp knife, cut into about 1-inch pieces and serve.

Vegetables

I want to encourage people to eat a lot of vegetables – you need them to create a balanced meal – but they don't have to be boring. In Japanese cuisine there are many ways of preparing vegetable dishes – raw, boiled, sautéed, simmered, pickled, dressed with a sesame sauce or simply grilled. However you prepare them, these dishes should be prepared with the same care and attention as you would give to the main dish – they are just as important and help to create a balance of color, nutrition and taste.

One important feature of Japanese cooking is the emphasis it places on seasonality, and this is particularly applicable to vegetable dishes. Get to know which seasons are best for which vegetables in your country. For example, in Japan summer is associated with the best eggplants, cucumbers, tomatoes and pumpkins, whereas potatoes, cabbage, green beans and bamboo shoots are best eaten in spring. This may be different in the country where you live so it's worth finding out when particular vegetables are at their best. If you eat vegetables in season you will find an amazing improvement in flavor.

Although salads are not a part of traditional Japanese cuisine we have now heartily embraced the concept from overseas. In restaurants most western-style meals come with a side salad, and Japanese supermarkets now sell a huge range of fresh vegetable produce.

A final point with vegetables is not to overcook them. Like the Italians and French, we like our vegetables crisp-tender, so that we can appreciate and enjoy their natural flavor and texture.

Carrot & Tuna Salad

Everyone enjoys a salad, and this one can be served either as a starter or with a main course. Carrots are often used in stews and in non-Japanese dishes. This carrot recipe has proved to be one of my most popular. I think it is because carrots and tuna just work so well together. The other reason is that carrots are better if they are lightly cooked – even for a salad. I recommend using a microwave to cook the carrots as they leave the carrots still very crispy and tasty – difficult to achieve if you boil them.

(Serves 4)
3 medium carrots, peeled
¼ cup finely chopped onion
1 teaspoon chopped garlic
1 tablespoon sunflower or vegetable oil
3 oz. canned tuna

Dressing:
2 tablespoons white wine vinegar
1 tablespoon mustard (preferably French
   whole grain mustard)
salt and pepper to taste
soy sauce to taste

1 First cut the carrots into about 2-inch thin juliennes.
2 Put them into a bowl suitable for the microwave and mix in the onion, garlic and sunflower oil. Cover and microwave on medium for 1–1½ minutes.
3 Once the carrots are lightly cooked add the drained tuna and then the dressing and mix well.
4 Serve hot or cold.
5 Please note you can increase the amounts for this recipe, but when you microwave the carrots I find it is better to only do this amount at any one time.

Warm Eggplant Salad
Nasu no salad

Eggplants are very popular in Japan and often feature on restaurant menus or in home cooking in one delicious way or another. In fact, Japanese seasonings work very well with eggplants, especially sesame, as you will discover when you try this recipe.

(Serves 4)
about 12 oz. eggplant

Sesame Sauce:
2½ tablespoons superfine sugar
2 tablespoons soy sauce
1 tablespoon sake
1 tablespoon rice vinegar
2 tablespoons ground sesame seeds
2 tablespoons sesame paste or tahini
   or unsweetened peanut butter

20g myoga – if available – or chopped
   green onions or shallots
5 shiso leaves or a mix of fresh mint
   and basil leaves

Ingredients Note:
Although myoga is sometimes called Japanese ginger it tastes nothing like ginger. So for this recipe I suggest you substitute green onions or shallots. Japanese eggplants are smaller than those commonly found in Europe, so you may need to quarter the eggplants lengthwise instead of halving them.

1 Chop off the eggplant stem and cut in half lengthwise. Soak in water for around 5 minutes, then drain and wipe dry. Place the halved eggplant on paper towels on a microwave-safe plate, cover and cook for 3–4 minutes. Let stand for a few minutes. Cut into long strips and then squeeze to get rid of excess water.

2 To make the sauce: add the seasoning to the sesame paste in the order listed above and mix.

3 Slice the myoga finely, rinse and drain, then slice again in half. Cut the shiso leaves in half lengthwise then into ⅛–inch strips.

4 Place the eggplant on a dish and add the sauce, coating it well. Then scatter the myoga and shiso leaves on top.

Salad with Sesame-Flavored Tofu Dressing

I like to use this sesame-flavored tofu sauce as an alternative to French dressing to liven up a plain salad. Because it's protein-rich, a salad dressed in this way can become a substantial part of a meal. The dressing works well on cooked or raw vegetables.

(Serves 4)
2 small carrots
4 oz. fresh green asparagus
2 oz. snow peas
several lettuce leaves
sesame-flavored tofu dressing (see below)
a handful of coarsely ground sesame
seeds to garnish

(Serves 4)
1 (12.3-oz.) box soft silken tofu
4 tablespoons sesame paste,
    or tahini or unsweetened peanut butter
1 tablespoon soy sauce
2 tablespoons superfine sugar
2 tablespoons mirin
¼ cup dashi or fish stock
salt

1 Chop the carrots into 2-inch matchsticks. Remove the woody part and any small outside leaves from the asparagus. Prepare the snow peas by removing any strings, and remove ends if necessary.

2 Cook the three vegetables separately so they are just cooked but still retain their bite, and plunge immediately into ice-cold water for five minutes to chill. Drain well and dry on paper towels.

3 Cut the asparagus diagonally into ½-inch pieces and each snow pea into 3 or 4 pieces. Tear the lettuce into fairly large pieces.

4 Combine all the vegetables in a bowl or on a deep plate and pour the sesame sauce over them. Sprinkle the ground sesame seeds on top.

Sesame-Flavored Tofu Dressing

(Goma fumi tofu sauce)

1 Drain the tofu and wrap it in paper towels to remove excess water.

2 Mix the sesame paste, soy sauce, sugar, mirin and dashi stock together in a bowl. Break the tofu into small pieces with your hands and add to the bowl. Mix lightly and season with salt.

French Beans and Asparagus Chili Style

Sayaingen to Asupara no Kinpira fu

I like using chilies in dishes like this and have found that it works very well with these particular vegetables. However, you can also try it with potatoes, carrots or anything you fancy. If you parboil the vegetables before you use them, it reduces their water content and keeps them crispy.

(Serves 4)
9 oz. asparagus
8 oz. French beans
2 tablespoons olive oil
1-2 teaspoons finely chopped
   dried red chili to taste
3 tablespoons soy sauce

1 Chop off the woody part and strip any side leaves from the asparagus and remove ends from the beans. Cook them in boiling water until just cooked but still with a bite to them, then soak in chilled water.

2 When cooled, drain, then pat dry the beans and asparagus. Cut the asparagus into 3 and slice lengthwise and cut the French beans in half.

3 Heat the olive oil in a frying pan or a wok and lightly fry the vegetables. Add the chopped red chili and soy sauce, quickly fry and serve.

Green Beans with Black Sesame Sauce

I am really happy when I have some good sesame seeds to cook with. I am also happy when I can use the natural colors of the ingredients to create an impact. The black sesame seeds used in this recipe make this simple dish quite striking.

(Serves 4)
8 oz. green beans
¼ cup roasted black sesame seeds
2 tablespoons superfine sugar
½ tablespoon mirin
1 tablespoon soy sauce

1 String the beans and cut in half lengthwise and then in half again. Parboil for a few minutes, taking care to remove before they soften. Drain and soak in iced water for a few minutes, drain again and pat dry.

2 In a large mortar lightly crush the sesame seeds. Add the sugar, mirin and soy sauce and mix to a smooth paste.

3 Add the green beans into the mortar and toss, making sure that the beans are all well covered with the dressing. I think that it's better to mix the beans and sauce by hand for the best results.

Green Beans Mixed with Ground Meat
Ingenno Hikiniku Itame

This dish with its sweet and spicy taste is perfect with rice. It's delicious even when served cold.

(Serves 4)
1 lb. green beans
3 tablespoons garlic and onion oil
   (see Ingredients Note)
8 oz. ground pork
½ teaspoon red chili peppers, finely sliced
   and seeds removed
3 tablespoons soy sauce
½ teaspoon superfine sugar

Ingredients Note:
To make the garlic and onion oil: put 2 cloves of thinly sliced garlic, ¾ cup thinly sliced onion, 1 cup finely chopped green onion and 2 cups of sunflower oil in a wok and heat over low heat. When the green onions turn dark brown remove from the heat. While the oil is still hot, filter using a paper filter – taking care not to burn yourself. Leave it to cool. Make sure that the oil is cold before pouring into a bottle for future use. Please only use the oil while it still smells fresh.

1 String the green beans and cut diagonally into 3 pieces. Parboil for a few minutes, removing while still slightly firm. Soak in iced water and drain. Squeeze to remove any excess water.
2 Heat 1 tablespoon of the garlic and onion oil in a wok and fry the pork. Add the red chili pepper and fry. Season with 2 tablespoons of soy sauce and the sugar.
3 Add a further 2 tablespoons garlic and onion oil and add the green beans and mix. Season quickly with a tablespoon of soy sauce and serve.

Spinach Ohitashi Style
Horenso no Ohitashi

Spinach prepared in this style is simple but unbelievably tasty.

(Serves 4)
10 oz. fresh spinach
3 tablespoons roasted sesame seeds
nori seaweed to taste
dried fish flakes to taste
soy sauce to taste

1 Parboil the spinach until just wilted but not cooked through. Chill for a few minutes in iced water and then squeeze it well to get rid of excess water. Chop into 1-inch pieces.

2 Squeeze the spinach again then lightly separate out the leaves.

3 Divide into two piles and place on a serving plate. Crush the seaweed into small flakes and sprinkle on one pile of spinach and put the dried fish flakes on the other. Add a little soy sauce.

Hijiki Seaweed Salad

I don't understand why so many westerners feel so nervous about eating seaweed – it's tasty, healthy and nonfattening. In Japanese cooking we use many types of seaweed but this is one of my favorites. Be careful not to oversoak the hijiki seaweed and make it too soft. I have suggested using particular vegetables in this salad with the hijiki seaweed – these are ones I always have in my fridge. Use whatever type you have available.

(Serve 4)
⅓ oz. hijiki seaweed (dried)
a variety of vegetables: lettuce, celery, carrots,
    cucumber and onions to taste.

Anchovy Dressing:
2 canned anchovy fillets
2 tablespoons sunflower or vegetable oil
1 tablespoon wine vinegar
a little superfine sugar
pepper
1 teaspoon soy sauce

1 Soak the hijiki seaweed in warm water for about 10 minutes, drain well and dry. Cut it into short pieces if they are too long.
2 Cut the vegetables into thin strips, soak them in cold water for 5 minutes, drain and pat dry.
3 Mince the anchovy and mix it with the other ingredients for the dressing.
4 Mix the hijiki and cut vegetables and put on a serving dish. Pour over the anchovy dressing just before eating.

Desserts & Drinks

In the past, mostly we would finish a meal with some fresh fruit, but nowadays many Japanese enjoy something sweeter after eating, so serving desserts is now commonplace.

In fact I have always enjoyed serving dessert for my family, but never commercially made ones as I find them too sweet. Although many more homes than in the past now have an oven, many women still don't like using them, so I have developed dessert recipes that can be made without baking.

We have adopted many desserts from overseas and now regard many of them as being our own. Certainly, many looking at Japanese versions of cheesecake or tiramisu might find them quite altered, especially in the size of the serving. So, to keep to the spirit of Japanese cuisine, when you serve dessert serve less than you usually would – I think it should be just a taste rather than something that fills you up. Think small!

Petal-Style Crepes

I think that many of my Japanese readers were surprised to find this recipe in my magazine. They always assumed that these traditional crepes are too difficult to make at home, until they tried this recipe. The crepe itself is a beautiful pale pink color, created with a little food coloring. The filling is a sweet red bean paste which is a common ingredient in Japanese and Chinese desserts and is usually sold canned in Asian supermarkets. If you can't find it you can make your own quite simply – see my note below. Sweet things like this are always served with Japanese green tea or Chinese jasmine tea.

(For 10 crepes)
1 cup all-purpose flour
1 cup water
1 teaspoon sugar
salt
sunflower or vegetable oil
a few drops of red food coloring
a little water
10 tablespoons sweetened bean paste

Ingredients Note:
If you can't find bean paste you can easily make it yourself. Soak adzuki beans overnight and then cook until soft, then mash. Add sugar to taste and stir vigorously over a low heat until the sugar has dissolved.

1 Put the flour, water, sugar and salt into a bowl and whisk well until smooth, then add a teaspoon of sunflower oil.

2 Mix a few drops of the food coloring with a little water, and add to the batter little by little, until it turns a pale cherry blossom color (be careful not to use too much coloring – you don't want a lurid pink). Leave to stand for 30 minutes.

3 Heat a spoonful of oil in a small frying pan on a low heat so the surface is well oiled, then gently wipe off any excess with paper towels. Pour in enough batter to make a thin crepe 4-5 inches in diameter, tilting the pan to ensure that it is even. Leave the crepe to cook on one side, then turn over and cook briefly. Repeat as before until you have used all the batter. Leave the crepes to cool.

4 Take 1 tablespoon of the bean paste, shape into a ball and place in the center of each crepe. Fold in half, then fold again as in the photo.

5 The best way to serve these crepes is to place a couple on a small dish for each person; if possible find one that complements the pink color.

Steamed Cream Cheese Muffins

This recipe is so simple that you can easily make these muffins for breakfast in the morning. As they are light and sweet they are also good for afternoon tea.

(Serves 4)
¼ cup cream cheese
½ tablespoon white wine
1 tablespoon heavy cream
1 tablespoon sunflower or vegetable oil
vanilla extract to taste
2 medium-size eggs
¼ cup sugar
½ cup all-purpose flour
½ teaspoon baking powder

Possible toppings:
Buttercream
Mix 3 tablespoons of superfine sugar with
3 tablespoons softened, unsalted butter
until it becomes pale. Slowly add 3 tablespoons
of heavy cream, mixing as you go.

Peanut Cream
Add 2 tablespoons superfine sugar to 6
tablespoons of heavy cream. Whisk for
5–6 minutes until thick and add 4 tablespoons
of peanut butter (crunchy type). Mix well.

To make the cream cheese mixture:

1 First prepare the dishes: line 4 large ramekin dishes with waxed paper. You can either cut pieces to size, or simply press paper into the dish to create a creased paper effect.

2 Put the cream cheese and white wine in a microwave-safe container and cover. Microwave on medium for 20 seconds.

3 Take out and whisk until it becomes creamy.

4 Add the heavy cream, sunflower oil and vanilla extract. Mix well.

5 In a separate bowl beat the eggs and add the sugar. Whisk until it thickens.

6 Add the flour and baking powder to the egg and sugar mixture, mixing lightly and then add the cream cheese.

7 Half fill each ramekin dish with batter and cover loosely with plastic wrap, allowing plenty of room for the mixture to rise.

8 Microwave on low for 5 minutes, then microwave on medium for 1½ minutes, or until tops spring back when pressed.

9 Turn the muffins out while they are still hot and remove the waxed paper. Add topping, if desired.

Mont Blanc–Style Dessert

The "Mont Blanc" style of cakes is very popular in Japan and these mountain-shaped cakes can be found in most cake shops. They are usually made from cooked, puréed chestnuts, but I think that they are just as good made with sweet potato.

The important point is that the little mound of purée is decorated with more purée which has been put through a potato ricer or grinder, to create thick shreds or ribbons – the end result should look a little like that famous mountain!

(Serves 4)
1 large sweet potato
3–4 tablespoons sugar
1 tablespoon butter
1 beaten egg yolk (see Egg Safety, page 66)
¼ cup heavy cream
1 tablespoon rum
1 teaspoon mirin
cinnamon powder to taste
powdered sugar to taste

1 Peel the sweet potato and cut into pieces just slightly bigger than bite-size. As you cut, drop them immediately into a bowl of water to prevent them discoloring. When ready to cook, drain the pieces and pat them dry.

2 Put some paper towels in a microwave-safe bowl and add the sweet potato. Cover and microwave for 5–6 minutes.

3 Remove from the microwave, take off the plastic wrap and mash. Add the sugar, butter and half the egg yolk (you will need the other half later) and mix well. Leave the mixture to cool.

4 In a separate bowl, lightly whisk the cream. Fold the whisked cream into the mashed potato then add the rum and mix again.

5 The potato mixture should now be quite stiff and easy to handle. Form half of the mix into eight egg-shaped portions. Place on a baking pan and glaze with a mixture made of the remaining half egg yolk and the mirin.

6 Place under a medium hot broiler until they turn golden brown. Leave to cool.

7 Place two portions per person on individual plates.

8 Finally, take the remaining half of the mixture and put it in a potato ricer. Squeeze potato shreds over each portion, dividing it equally. Sprinkle each "mountain" with the cinnamon powder and powdered sugar.

Watermelon Sorbet
Suika no Sherbert

Watermelon is a wonderful fruit. It feeds the senses with its green shell, red flesh and black seeds. It is also fantastic on a hot summer's day when its watery and crispy flesh is just what you need to refresh yourself. However, I think this sorbet is even more refreshing than the original fruit.

(Serves 5~6)
3 tablespoons sugar
3 tablespoons water
2 lbs. watermelon flesh
1 tablespoon lemon juice
1 tablespoon kirsch liquor

1 Mix together the sugar and water in a microwave-safe container. Put in a microwave and cook for 3 minutes on medium without covering. Leave to cool.
2 Take the watermelon pulp and remove the seeds then mash the pulp with a balloon whisk. Add the cooled syrup, lemon juice and kirsch to taste and mix well.
3 Pour into a stainless steel square mold and cover with plastic wrap. Freeze for a couple of hours.
4 To serve, scrape the sorbet into icy granules with a spoon, and serve in a dish that shows off the beautiful color.

Green Tea Jelly
Macha Jelly

Once you eat this dessert, you will become addicted to it. This is a must-have Japanese dessert! The slightly bitter taste of the green tea powder and the condensed milk are a perfect combination. I love making this jelly so that it only just sets so don't be surprised at how soft it is.

(Serves 4)
The Jelly:
2 teaspoons plain gelatin powder
1⅓ tablespoons green tea powder (macha powder)
4 tablespoons superfine sugar
¼ cup boiling water
1½ cups tap water

The Milk Sauce:
½ cup sweetened condensed milk
½ cup whole milk

some sweetened red adzuki beans to taste

Ingredients Note:
You can buy cans of red adzuki beans in most Asian food shops (see page 149, Petal-Style Crepes)

1 Put 1½ tablespoons of water in a microwave-safe bowl and add the gelatin and mix well. Cover and microwave on medium for 10 seconds until the gelatin has fully dissolved.

2 In a separate bowl mix the green tea powder and sugar.
Add the hot water little by little to make a paste.
Then add a further 1½ cups of tap water and mix well.

3 Add the gelatin liquid to the tea and mix it in quickly. Pour into a mold and refrigerate to set, stirring occasionally to prevent the mixture from separating.

4 To make the milk sauce, combine condensed milk and whole milk. Once the jelly has set scoop out and serve using a large spoon. Pour over the milk sauce and top with adzuki beans to taste.

Tea

It is amazing how Japanese green tea has taken the world by storm. Not so long ago it would be inconceivable to think that you could find it in most supermarkets internationally. Now you can find green tea bags almost everywhere and the health benefits from drinking the tea are well recognized.

Green tea (o-cha) is taken all day in Japan. It is impossible to have a meal without it. In restaurants your teacup is constantly topped up, at no extra cost. In hotel rooms, you will always find a kettle and green tea. At any meeting you will automatically be presented with a cup of tea. Tea is everywhere!

Outside of Japan it's probably easier to find tea bags than loose tea, but most Japanese, including me, prefer the taste of tea made with fresh tea leaves. I come from one of the major tea growing areas of Japan, Shizuoka Prefecture, and I cannot imagine using anything other than good, fresh green tea leaves. If you can find loose tea then try it in preference to bags.

O-cha is easy to make, providing you follow a few simple rules.
1 Heat the teapot before putting the tea leaves in.
2 Don't use boiling water – the water should be around 120-160°F.
3 Japanese teapots are small and you should use around 2–3 teaspoons of tea per pot. Do not leave the tea for more than 2–3 minutes before pouring.
4 Pour the tea little by little into the cups so each cup has an equivalent color and taste.
5 Use the best tea you can afford. You can use the leaves again – use hotter water for the second and third use.

Our tea cups are quite small and without handles so be careful not to fill the cup too much or you will not be able to hold it until it has cooled down. A traditional style of cup comes in pairs — a large one for the man, and a smaller one for the woman. I have designed a modern version — a pair of cups of equal size. We have a wonderful range of cups and teapots, from fine china to chunky earthenware, and it's always fun deciding on which style to use.

Hojicha

Is most commonly drunk after meals. This tea has a wonderful nutty flavor as a result of the tea leaves being roasted. Although hojicha is more difficult to find than green tea you can easily make your own.

Take a handful of green tea leaves and put them in a wok or a frying pan and cook on a low heat, shaking from time to time. When the leaves change color, they're ready for use.

Iced Green Tea

Is a popular drink in summer. I love iced green tea. To make it, make the tea slightly stronger than usual. Make enough pots of tea to fill a pitcher, allow to cool, then add lots of ice cubes. Try it out on your friends and family during the summer.

Glossary

If you want to ask for things in Japanese (in a shop or restaurant) it is an easy language to pronounce as long as you remember to pronounce each letter individually and to keep the vowels pure: "A" as in apple, "I" as in ink, "U" as in put, "E" as in egg and "O" as in pot. It is not accented and in general no sound is lengthened more than others.

Ao-nori Dried, finely chopped seaweed. Often used on top of okonomiyaki.

Asari clams A small type of clam, common to Japan.

Bento Japanese lunchbox.

Bok Choy Sometimes spelled as pak choi or pak choy. A Chinese leafy green vegetable.

Chirimen Zansho Dried baby anchovies flavored with sweet soy sauce and sansho pepper.

Daikon Japanese radish, sometimes found in Asian shops called mooli.

Dashi Stock made from kombu and dried fish flakes (katsuo bushi). The basis of much of Japanese cooking.

Dashi no moto Instant dashi granules, available in Japanese stores.

Ginger Fresh ginger comes as a knobby root vegetable that needs to be peeled before use. It is frequently used in Japanese cooking, both fresh and pickled. There are two types of pickled ginger – the thin wafer thin slices eaten with sushi, (gari) and the red julienned version that is eaten with okonomiyaki and yakisoba (beni-shoga).

Harusame noodles Very fine translucent noodles made from mung bean starch, or more likely sweet potato or potato starch. The name means "spring rain" which they resemble.

Ichimi Togarashi Chili powder.

Katsuo Bushi Smoked and dried bonito fish that is shaved into very fine flakes before use. Used in many recipes, including dashi, it has a distinctive flavor.

Kinome The young leaves of the sansho plant. Not readily available in the west.

Kombu Kelp seaweed. Used to make dashi stock and in simmered foods.

Kombu cha powder Ground kombu used as a tea. It has a good strong salty flavor.

La Yu Chili oil, often used with Chinese dishes like gyoza.

Mentaiko The roe of the Alaska pollack or cod, salted and seasoned with chili pepper.

Mentsuyu A basic dipping sauce, usually made from dashi, soy sauce, salt and sugar.

Mirin A sweet alcoholic liquid used in cooking to tenderize and sweeten, and balance saltiness. An essential ingredient in Japanese cooking.

Miso A rich savory paste made from fermented soy beans, salt and grain (usually rice or barley). It keeps for years and is a protein-rich addition to many dishes. It's the essential ingredient in miso soup. Red miso (akamiso) is dark and high in protein and salt. White miso (shiromiso) is milder and sweeter and suitable for dressings. Medium (awase miso) is all-purpose, being a mix of red and white miso.

Mitsuba Its botanical name is *Cryptotaenia japonica* and it resembles flat-leaf parsley in appearance but not taste, being more aromatic and fragrant. Dried leaves are available.

Mizuna *Brassica campestris*. A leafy green, sometimes called pot-herb mustard.

Mushrooms Japan has a huge variety of mushrooms, many of which you cannot find overseas. Most commonly used is the shiitake (dark and round – a little like chestnut mushrooms). However, maitake, shimeji, eringi and enoki are all commonly used: they are usually available in clumps and differ mainly in color and thickness of the stalks.

Myoga The fragrant bud of a type of ginger plant, *Zingiber mioga*. Available pickled, but occasionally you can find the fresh bud in Asian stores. Ginger is not a substitute.

Negi Japan has a huge range of vegetables from the onion family. Naga negi and banno negi are the most common and are comparable to our green onions and leeks.

Nori Seaweed, most usually encountered as dried thin crisp sheets which are used to wrap around sushi.

Nira Garlic chives – very pungent and tasty.

Ponzu Soy Sauce A dipping sauce made from soy sauce and citrus juice, traditionally sudachi or yuzu, but nowadays also lemon.

Potato starch (katakuriko) Similar to cornstarch but stronger, so use a little more cornstarch if you cannot find potato starch.

Rice (kome) The botanical name for Japanese rice is *Oryza sativa japonica*. It is short-grained so sticks together and can be eaten with chopsticks.

Rice vinegar This commonly used vinegar is made from rice and is low in acidity and mild in flavor.

Sansho pepper Made from the ground seedpods of the prickly ash, slightly spicy with a hint of citrus. Sansho is closely related to Szechuan pepper, which is acceptable as a substitute.

Sake Japanese rice wine. Used to tenderize foods. Similar to a very dry sherry. Can be drunk hot or cold.

Sashimi Sliced fish that is eaten raw, so must be extremely fresh.

Sesame oil Toasted sesame oil has a strong flavor and is used in small amounts. It burns easily.

Sesame paste Japanese sesame paste is rich and smooth, being made from toasted sesame seeds. Tahini is an acceptable alternative, although less refined.

Sesame seeds In Japan sesame seeds are usually sold already toasted. Both black and white sesame seeds are available.

Shichimi Togarashi This is a frequently used mix of seven spices, including chili.

Shiso Sometimes known as perilla or beefsteak plant and part of the mint family. Its leaves look rather like nettle leaves and are very aromatic. It is used as a garnish with sashimi, or chopped and served with rice or in salads.

Shochu A colorless spirit distilled from grain or starch, such as potato, barley or millet.

Shokoshu A Chinese rice wine that has a stronger flavor than sake with a subtle undertone of herbs.

Somen Very fine white wheat noodles, usually eaten chilled in summer.

Soy sauce Made from soybeans, wheat and salt, soy sauce is the ubiquitous flavoring in Japanese cooking. The regular soy sauce (koikuchi) is readily available in the west. A thinner soy sauce (usukuchi) is lighter, but actually saltier, and used when you don't want to darken the appearance of the food too much.

Tarako Salted cod roe.

Tentsuyu Dipping sauce for tempura – it's a diluted version of mentsuyu, diluted with dashi and served hot.

To-Ban-Jan Chinese chili paste.

Tofu A curd made from coagulated soy milk. There are two main types of fresh tofu: soft or silken tofu (kinugoshidofu). This falls apart easily and is best eaten just as it is with soy sauce and ginger, but it's also good for dips and dressings. Firm tofu (momendofu) is the pressed curds and therefore firmer. This is good for cooking.

Wakame A mild and delicate seaweed. Available dried it quickly rehydrates and is a common addition to miso soup and salads.

Wasabi The ground root of what is often referred to as Japanese horseradish. This is the green paste served with sashimi and sushi. Extremely pungent it can be bought in tubes, or as a powder ready to mix with water.

Yuzu A Japanese citrus fruit used in many recipes.

Zaa Sai Chinese pickles – green, crunchy and nutty in flavor, which need to be rinsed of salt before using.

Sources

In addition to local Japanese and Asian food markets, the Internet offers an array of sources for hard-to-find ingredients. Below are just a few suggestions.

Amazon.com
www.Amazon.com/kitchens
Asian foods and cooking equipment

Asian Food Grocer
www.Asianfoodgrocer.com
Asian foods

Eden Foods
www.edenfoods.com
Asian foods

Joyce Chen Products
www.joycechen.com
Asian foods and cooking equipment

Kalustyan's
www.kalustyans.com
800-352-3451
Asian and other specialty ingredients

Kitazawa Seed Co.
P.O. Box 13220
Oakland, CA 94661
510-595-1188
510-595-1860 fax
Asian and other seeds